Enough
Already

An anthology of
Australian–Jewish writing

Edited by
Alan Jacobs

ALLEN & UNWIN

This project has been assisted by the Commonwealth
Government through the Australia Council, its arts
funding and advisory body.

First published in 1999 by
Allen & Unwin
9 Atchison Street, St Leonards NSW 1590 Australia
Phone: (61 2) 8425 0100
Fax: (61 2) 9906 2218
E-mail: frontdesk@allen-unwin.com.au
Web: http://www.allen-unwin.com.au

National Library of Australia
Cataloguing-in-Publication entry:

Enough Already: an anthology of Australian–Jewish writing.

  ISBN 1 86448 756 9.

  1. Jews—Australia—Literary collections. 2. Australian literature—
  Jewish authors. 3. Australian literature—20th century. I. Jacobs,
  Alan.

A820.808924

Set in 10/14 pt Janson Text by Bookhouse Digital, Sydney
Printed and bound by Australian Print Group, Maryborough, Victoria

10 9 8 7 6 5 4 3 2 1

Contents

Four Words

The first ever collection of Australian-Jewish fiction, *Shalom* (edited by Nancy Keesing), appeared twenty-one years ago, in 1978. Ten years later, during the Bicentenary, another anthology, *Pomegranates*, edited by Gael Hammer, was published. Both surveyed the rich Jewish literary tradition which had emerged in Australia from the nineteenth century and highlighted such luminaries as Pinchas Goldhar, Herz Bergner, Judah Waten, David Martin and Nancy Keesing.

Another decade has elapsed. In the interim, a significant body of Jewish writers born post-war has evolved, mainly in Sydney and Melbourne. For some time I have toyed with the idea of showcasing these writers in a new anthology. Writers of my own (Baby Boomer) generation, as well as those of Generation X.

Shalom featured the talents of new writers in the seventies, such as Fay Zwicky and Morris Lurie. In fact these two were the youngest writers in the collection, though both born pre-war. Even though *Pomegranates* included a small number of younger writers, such as Rosa Safransky, Lily Brett and Serge Liberman, a collection focusing *solely* on writers born after the Second World War has never been attempted.

I believe such a collection is both timely and valuable for a number of reasons. For one thing, the proliferation of contemporary Jewish writing is a new phenomenon. In 1978, Nancy Keesing lamented, in the introduction of *Shalom*, that 'there are not, and never have been, many Australian-Jewish writers of fiction'. This is certainly not the case today as this anthology attests. Furthermore, many of the writers born post-war concentrate on a variety of issues and themes far different from those which concerned earlier generations of Jewish writers in Australia.

One issue or theme that comes readily to mind is that of the Holocaust, more particularly the recording of the experiences, obsessions and angst of descendants of Holocaust survivors. This is certainly one of the dominant themes among this generation of writers, though by no means the only one. A second is the search for one's Jewish roots. This issue seems to have undergone a renaissance with the emergence of multiculturalism in this country in the last ten or fifteen years. And yet another, which is evident from many of the writers in this anthology, is a father obsession, an overturning of the stereotype that the mother has a monopoly as the dominant influence on the Jewish child.

Neither of the previously published anthologies explored what I would call 'the edges' of Jewish writing in Australia. In this collection I have purposely sought not only writers who identify as Jews and who concentrate on Jewish themes, but also those who are Jewish but for whom Judaism acts as a minor or negligible force in their lives. What are their concerns? To what extent does Judaism inform their writing, even though it might not appear in the content?

I have borrowed the Nazi definition, for want of a better term, of Jewish identity. Thus, I have included writers who are only partly Jewish and those who may not be Jewish *Halachic*-ly (according to the Jewish religion), but who are willing to admit that they have an element of Jewish blood in their background. And are willing to write about it. Such writers as Dorothy Porter (paternal Jewish grandmother), Brian Castro (paternal Jewish grandfather) and Judy Horacek, whose Jewish father, as a result of the Holocaust, was raised as a Catholic, are obviously not Jews by strict religious definition. But I believe that their literary references to this background make them valid for inclusion in this collection.

If there is a theme to this anthology, it is a loose one of identity. Among the authors represented most come from a European (if not Holocaust survivor) background. One or two come from Anglo-Jewish stock. Andrea Goldsmith, for example, is a fifth-generation Australian Jew. While the Jewish community in Australia today (particularly in Sydney and Melbourne) is far more diverse in terms of its cultural composition than has previously been the case, few significant writers from the more recently arrived members of our community have as yet emerged. There are obvious reasons for this.

Since the seventies, relatively large waves of Jewish immigration have occurred from the former Soviet Union and from South Africa. And in the eighties, young Israelis began to travel to Australia and some have settled here, as have Jewish migrants from South America. These new elements in the Jewish community tend to keep to themselves at first until slowly some integration with the older, more established community occurs. It is a pattern which began with the arrival of Polish Jews in the 1920s, continued with German and Austrian Jewish refugees before the war, and culminated with the relatively huge influx of Holocaust survivors in the late forties and early fifties. In time the nature of the Jewish community metamorphosed, as it continues to do.

In terms of literary integration, Pinchas Goldhar and Herz Bergner are obvious exceptions. Not only were they first-generation writers on the Australian–Jewish scene but they had an impact on many succeeding writers. Perhaps Judah Waten and Serge Liberman could be included in this group though both came to Australia as youngsters.

Hopefully the next anthology of Australian-Jewish writing will include Russians, South Africans and others, or their descendants, drawing on new and different experiences and themes.

The writing of fiction and poetry has always been a valued part of Jewish culture and tradition. The ongoing chronicling of the Australian-Jewish experience through its literary outpouring is, I believe, a very important task. Jewish writers have always held up a mirror to our collective Jewish soul, monitoring it and providing constant, if sometimes unpleasant, feedback. Australian-Jewish writers are no different. The Australian-Jewish experience is today rich and varied, and is also maturing now that Jews feel more confident and secure about their place in Australia. A similar phenomenon occurred in the United States thirty or forty years ago, yielding many writers like Philip Roth and Saul Bellow, who are now accepted as part of the mainstream culture.

The healthy and significant body of writing in this anthology reflects this growing maturity as well as the elevation of some of our more important contemporary Jewish writers to national prominence.

Alan Jacobs
1999

Only Connect: Musings of an Australian Jew

Andrea Goldsmith

Andrea Goldsmith is a Melbourne-based writer and a fifth generation Australian Jew. She has published four novels, Facing the Music *(1994),* Modern Interiors *(1991) and* Gracious Living *(1989). Her most recent novel,* Under the Knife *(Allen & Unwin, 1998), combines modern tragedy with a feral biography, and is fuelled by an obsessive love.*

WHEN I WAS A child, there were regular discussions around the family dinner table on the issue of Australian Jew or Jewish Australian. Which was to have the authority of the noun? Jew or Australian? And which, by default, would be allocated secondary status? The way the problem was posed, I now realise, set the identities up as mutually incompatible—not a simple case of subjugation, rather the dominance of one tended to obliterate the other.

The concept of the hyphenate Jew is not new. In the essays of Thorstein Veblen and Hannah Arendt, and the literature of such writers as Henry Roth, Saul Bellow and Bernard Malamud the hyphenate Jew is a powerful presence, indeed, it is common to Jews around the world. However, in my own case, until very recently, my Jewish side took precedence almost to the exclusion of the Australian. This was not the triumph of one over the other, but a necessity. Being a Jew set me apart from other Australians. Being a Jew inspired guilt, insecurity and fear. The Jew in me required vigilance, the Jew in me required defending. *The Jew in me*, but the wrong sort of Jew. So I set out to repair it, constructing what I believed was the only acceptable identity for a Jew in the aftermath of the Holocaust.

When first I conceived my Jewish quest it was vague and intellectually shapeless. A Cook's tour of the concentration camps. Auschwitz, of course, and Treblinka, Bergen-Belsen, Theresienstadt, Buchenwald and Dachau. It is hard to remember exactly, it was all so long ago. And in the interim, so many books read, films seen, personal testimonies heard, so much gathering to this Australian-born heart places and events external to my own shamefully safe Jewish history. I thought the only authentic definition of a Jew in the twentieth century was to be found in the horrors of the Holocaust. Now I wonder whether it was a lack of imagination, or perhaps too much of it—and I am a fiction writer after all—that propelled me to Europe.

Over the years, the journey became more defined and at the same time more diverse. I needed to see the site of the Warsaw ghetto and the Polish towns where Jewish life had thrived for centuries. I had to linger in squares where synagogues once stood, and wander ancient cemeteries searching for derelict Jewish graves. And the first ghetto, the Ghetto Nuova in Venice, surely I should see that. And the little town of Slonim that bounced back and forth between Russia and Poland over the centuries, the town that bears the name of my grandfather who travelled to Australia at the turn of the century, I should visit there too. And the other concentration camp sites, their very abundance an eloquent reminder of the efficiency of hate, these would need to be seen. And the tasteful memorials of prowling guilt that were springing up across Europe marking this massacre or that pogrom, more of them as the passage of time conveniently reshaped memory, they should be included too. Every book I read expanded my trip. Then I saw Claude Lanzmann's film *Shoah*, and the journey spilled into years. There were train tracks to travel and ageing faces to see; there were thinly disguised protests to hear and the courage to stand my ground when confronted by people who were, and remain, perfectly happy for my sort to be destroyed. You can still look death in the eye, thirty, forty, even fifty years on. Indeed, if the *Shoah* proved one thing, the Jew will always be aware of the pale eyes of death.

I read my books, I went to films, I spoke to survivors and the children of survivors, and the journey grew. Bear witness, Primo Levi said. I had to bear witness and I wasn't even there.

A Jew, a fifth-generation Australian through three of my grandparents, raised in a family that observed *Shabbat*, that went to *shul* regularly if not assiduously, that did not keep *kosher* but would never eat pork. An Australian-born Jew who attended a Methodist girls' school, who made the annual pilgrimage each Christmas to the Myer window display, who would have followed Australian rules football if it had been more to her taste, and as homeless as if she had just landed on these shores. It simply did not make sense. I went to live in Carlton, in the block adjacent to where my grandfather's family lived when they first arrived in Australia. 'It took us decades to move away from there,' my cousin said. 'Why do you want to go back?'

But I was not going back. I was collecting memories, I was searching for history, I was trying to construct foundations to what I was increasingly experiencing as an illegitimate life. I wanted to find a home, I wanted the certainty of belonging, I wanted to be authenticated as an

Australian Jew. And isn't this what we all want when we search for roots?

I did not find home in late twentieth-century Carlton with its renovated terrace houses, its students and academics and labour lawyers. I did not find it in the resonances of Jewish life that still remained: old Mr Pose the cucumber man, or the former North Carlton synagogue, or the building that used to house the Yiddish theatre. Oddly, I found a greater sense of home with the Italians, the migrants who came to Carlton after the Jews whose culture still thrived there. I found a home, but it was not mine.

So I gathered up my emptiness and returned to Europe. How is it possible to dream of places never seen? The craggy monuments of Treblinka and the railway track leading to Auschwitz; and running helplessly through foreign streets chased by shadowy men with huge mouths, their black boots thundering on the flagstones. How could I dream of these things when I was never there? I read about the nightmares of children of survivors. In texture, sometimes even in the images, they were similar to mine. My parents were born in Melbourne, they had no family in Europe during the war, why then did I have the nightmares? Dreams, I read, fill in the gaps of the waking consciousness. How fitting, I thought, for a Jew to find her identity in the shadows of night.

The Jew as the archetypal outsider, it strikes even the most privileged of us. And guilt over not having suffered enough. And homelessness. And the need for roots.

I used to think it would have been easier if I had been born in a different country, one with a longer documented history and a different cultural landscape. Five generations of Australianness did not provide an antidote to the otherness of Jewishness, and the Australianness on offer seemed such an ill fit. But if I had been born in a country where I could trace not five, but ten or twenty generations, then, I thought, I would belong. As if sanctuary were a place. As for Israel, I visited only briefly: the politics, the landscape, and most particularly its unselfconscious Jewishness marked me out as a different Jew. No comfort to be found there.

And I thought it would be easier if I were a different Jew in Australia. In this country, the stereotypical Jew has a European background. Who was I with my fifth-generation Australian heritage and not one relative killed in the Holocaust?

Only much later did it occur to me that the search for identity is the search for certainty. A common enough human desire, but pure illusion. And for those with minds attuned not to facts and truths, but possibilities and the maddening chameleonics of meaning, to hunger for certainty is surely to starve.

It is the journey that matters, indeed, there is nothing but the journey, and for this Jew, like so many others, it has become a word-journey, a textual journey. I've not visited the concentration camps, nor the sites of the *shtetls*, I've not said *Kaddish* over crumbling Jewish graves, nor stood my ground against dogged enemies. I've read books. My entire journey travelled in books, in words, in what is portable and invisible, what can be carried when the next pogrom strikes. Identity, that mysterious, elusive, mutable texture of being, finds a natural home in the hidden, elusive, encoded world of language. I am no Talmudic scholar,

I don't even understand Hebrew, but this excavation of identity is Talmudic in quality. And it is a process that connects me to others: different Jews from different places and different times. Five generations will never be enough for anyone to find a home, but through books the opportunities are greatly increased.

And it is a home in uncertainty. Not the words, they are always there, neatly tattooed to the page. The uncertainty resides in the semantics, endless and clandestine, a boundless landscape for the wandering mind. Uncertainty, whether we like it or not, is the connective tissue of the human condition. As for the flight from meaning, it is nothing other than a desperate hurtling towards the brick wall of certainty.

I was thirty-two when I first read George Steiner's essay 'Our Homeland, the Text'. There are illuminated moments in every reader's life and for me this was one of them, as had been *Language and Silence* several years before. Steiner writes: 'In post-exilic Judaism, but perhaps earlier, active reading, answerability to the text on both the meditative-interpretative and the behavioural levels, is the central motion of personal and national homecoming.' He was referring to the *Torah* ('…wherever in the world a Jew reads and meditates Torah *is* the true Israel') but I recognised its wider application for an Australian-born Jew searching for her roots, a Jew who lacked all the acceptable accoutrements of Jewishness. I did not even 'look Jewish' as so many non-Jews felt obliged to tell me. I think they meant it as a compliment, but it simply added to my shame.

The book. The word. Its miraculous survival. Its convenient portability. The text provides private connections to help construct the public Jew. It is, according to Steiner, 'the instrument of exilic survival'. Orthodox Judaism holds no attraction for me; the traditional observance of Judaism is not where I locate my Jewishness. Yet I feel *none the less* a Jew, *am* none the less a Jew. I have chosen my own texts, untutored choices and deliberately contemptuous of order. It is not that they keep me Jewish, rather they build the Jew and support the Jew where religious observance is not an option and secular culture turns a suspicious eye.

The Jew of the Diaspora feels always in the spotlight. Don't draw attention to yourself, European Jews were told when they first arrived in Australia. And from my own father I learned that Jews had to be better citizens than non-Jews; that when a Jewish Australian committed a wrong it had repercussions for all Jews. It is not surprising then that so many Jews congregate behind the protective mantle of orthodoxy and community. The non-observant Jew is excoriated in Orthodox circles, the non-observant Jew would be barred at the *Yeshiva* door, yet for the observant and non-observant alike, the text prevails.

We Jews stand buried in paper; the stockpile grows even while our allotted three score years and ten contract. Home for the Jew is where the books are, raucous and uncomfortable, vibrant and enduring. Finally, I thought, I have resolved this identity conundrum. But there were nudgings from the other side of the equation; the Australian in me, so long neglected, was hustling for attention.

My Jewishness I have found in books, my Australian-ness, when it existed at all, was little more than a whiff of eucalyptus. As I was the wrong sort of Jew, so I was the wrong sort of Australian. It is not simply that I'm small and bookish, that I don't care for sport and hate the heat, more crucially I've never been convinced by the Australian cultural myths of mateship, egalitarianism and a fair go. Australia has its hierarchies like everywhere else. It is easy to use tokens—the occasional Asian face or black face in the corridors of power—as evidence of a happy melting pot, but these faces stand out because of their difference. It is only when we stop noticing that we'll have something to boast about.

I've never felt a sense of belonging here. If it were not for the fact that my mother's face is stamped on my own, I would think myself a changeling, dumped by accident in this part of the world. And I am urban, flagrantly urban. I find comfort in the noise and crowd of a big city. Country towns are quaint, but I visit them as I might a theme park, gazing always from the outside. As for the wide open spaces, I hate the exposure, there's nowhere to hide, I want to scurry home to the shadows and bluestone barriers of Melbourne.

American Jews such as Alfred Kazin, Saul Bellow and Henry Roth have cemented their Jewish identity with New York, but my connection with Melbourne, although strong, provides me with safe anonymity, not belonging. I experience a similar sense when visiting any large city of the world. I've memorised the script for the archetypal white Australian and can provide a creditable performance for the people I meet overseas, but the fact remains they are more likely to have seen the Australian landscape with its unique flora and fauna than have I, and will pronounce on Australia's icons with a warmth and appreciation I do not feel.

So little time on my sense or lack of being Australian; I wonder now if I found it all too difficult. Being Australian-born seemed to compound the problems of my Jewishness. And the Australian on offer made me uneasy. I have a horror of nationalism—what Jew doesn't? The jingo-istic soundings of the past decade or so have been as dangerous as they have been loud. My Jewishness has taught me not simply the value of pluralism but its necessity; my Jewishness has me searching for the outsiders in the crowd rather than looking at the crowd itself. I have resented the pretence of inclusion when the Australian 'she'll be right mate' attitude means that no effort towards connection ever need be made. Then there's the Australian championing of celebrity, with a pantheon cluttered with golfers, cricketers and footballers and rarely an artist or intellectual included. Indeed, anti-intellectualism is integral to the Australian package. I have resisted the Australian on offer, and yet have made no attempt to seek out alternatives.

Then came the baleful pantings of Pauline Hanson amid nonsensical platitudes that everyone has a right to their opinion; and the lambasting of native title and Howard's ten-point plan. (Can anything be resolved in a ten-point plan?) Then a series of actions, some deliberate others not, damaging Australia's relations with Asia and the Pacific, and finally the release of Ronald Wilson's report on the stolen children, *Bringing Them Home*. With each additional disaster I became more angry. So much of what I believed to be crucial to a humane society was being ignored or debunked. And it was not a Jewish anger, despite my values and ethics having been formed by my Jewishness, but rather an anger emanating from a deeply embedded idea of a possible Australia that was being permanently disabled. And then there was the shame, I was bristling with it. Suddenly I started to feel Australian.

Why now? Why not ten years ago during the bicentennial shenanigans? Why not when Bondy won the America's Cup? Why not with Kieran Perkins' win in the 1500-metres freestyle? The answer was obvious: all these were celebrity occasions buoyed along by national pride, of course they failed to move me. But now I was on the defensive, now I feared the loss of things I valued. My Jewishness, long protected and defended, was forging the Australian in me: the hyphenate Jew was finally emerging.

I signed petitions, I wrote letters to politicians, I engaged in heated and aggrieved conversations at trendy urban cafes. But I was not so foolish as to think this was political action, the excavation of identity never is. And then I went to the Northern Territory.

The trip had been planned months before and without any serious intent. I would see Australia's famous icons, take my photos, pick up some Australian tips to use in my archetypal Australian performances, and have a holiday. It would be like visiting Sydney, only less crowded. By the time the trip came about, the papers were full of Hanson, *Bringing Them Home* had just been released, and reconciliation was under threat. I took my anger, shame and disgust, I took my white sensibility and I went into Aboriginal Australia.

*

I see dispossession everywhere in Alice Springs, and a clinging to a culture under threat. There's a fist around my

Jewish heart. I want to join the groups of Aboriginal women and children, but have no right. I've never before felt my white Australianness so strenuously and I've never wanted it less. Why, I wonder, when I have identified so closely with other outsiders, have I not with Aboriginal Australians? Expulsion, massacre, genocide, eternal scapegoats: Jews and black Australians are equally experienced.

I drive out from Alice Springs. The road is straight, cutting a hard black line through a huge red disc of country. Astonishingly red, an out-of-this-world red. And small knobs of brush sprouting from the redness, and every now and then the flatness erupting into ancient rocky mounds clustered like smooth heads of old bald men. The effect is immediate: a stillness almost muscular in quality. Belonging, exposure, self-protection, all the words I associate with identity are scuttled. I don't understand, and yet I connect with a presence that is palpable. It is like leafing through an ancient manuscript written in an unfamiliar script and I soak it in.

The same sense the next day when walking the rim of Kings Canyon. My mind, so relentless in its search for meaning (to understand is, after all, to be armed), is stilled. And a presence or presences older than anything I've ever read. The rocky escarpments, the flanks of stark red rock, the caves, the crevasses, the huge beehive domes of neatly layered rock, all this is beyond my sort of knowledge.

I am confronted by Uluru. My books won't help me here. How, I wonder, can the unknown be so assertive, so intrusive, so obdurately present? I keep to the paths set by the Anangu people. I am a stranger, but do not feel an outsider, and, oddly, don't feel like a trespasser. I gaze upon the curved rocks of Kata Tjuta, see engraved on their huge smoothness dimples and caves, and feel with shocking clarity a sense of the sacred. And I breathe it in, this urban Jew walking on Aboriginal land, I breathe it in.

Later, Margorie, an Anangu elder, asks me what church I belong to. Her English is steeped in her own language and I struggle to understand. She tells me she is Lutheran, her husband a pastor. 'What church,' she says again. I tell her I am Jewish. We both laugh, black Australian and white Jew in a connection of sorts.

North to Kakadu and I am wanting to see the rock art. I had imagined it as a text to this strange and bizarre country. But something else happens when you gaze at a figure that is thousands of years old, its arms wide with stories, its very existence proclaiming a right to possession. Culture, ethics, spirituality, stubborn endurance and a respect for the land, all are revealed in these drawings. Not far from the site of the proposed Jabiluka mine, I look in astonishment at the sickness figure with his swollen joints. The painting is thousands of years old, yet the artist knew all about the sickness buried in this country. I gaze upon the all-powerful lightning man, and the rainbow serpent in her curved wisdom, and the marvellous Yawk Yawk who embody the union of land, animals, people, the law and spirit. For forty thousand years Aboriginal people have cemented their connection with the land. This is not a matter of certainty, but rather coherence, and it is, literally, awesome.

Later, I am told by an Aboriginal woman that Kakadu is so rich in food that the traditional landowners of the past needed to spend only a couple of hours every day hunting and gathering. The rest of the time was passed in the teaching and practice of culture and belief. A *Yeshiva* in the bush I find myself thinking, now that's a *Yeshiva* I'd like to attend.

Ronald Wilson's report on the stolen children referred to genocide. Many Jews objected to the term. But genocide does not require the efficiency of Nazi Germany; eugenics are slower than gas ovens, but just as effective. Children removed from their families and their spiritual and cultural roots; parents left with no children to pass their wisdom on to. Two incidences of genocide: different places, different times, different methods.

Jewishness and Judaism, to borrow Hannah Arendt's distinction, are not the same. I describe myself as a secular Jew, yet Jewish orthodoxy would consider that an oxymoron. I have a sense of the transcendent but I do not believe in God. Deprive Orthodox Jews of following the practices of their religion and they would still be Jewish, would still feel Jewish. Jewishness is not to be found in the observance of *kashrut* and *Shabbat*, nor in the respectful covering of the head. The observances, the practices of belief, so it seems to me, construct a sense of certainty by reducing the transcendent to human size. But if Jews were separated from the book, from words, what would happen then? Does the book for the Jew function as the land for the Aborigine?

When I returned to Melbourne my sense of myself as a Jew was not much changed, but for the first time I was aware of a connection to Australia struck from contact with a land and a people far older than we Jews. And it mixes well in me. I am no Jewish scholar and I'm downright ignorant of Aboriginal history and culture, I could be seen as a trespasser by both groups. And yet given that white Australia commences with a concentration camp on the one hand and attempted genocide on the other, to be a Jew and a defensive Australian demonstrates a certain logic.

The portable, rootless text has illuminated my Jewishness, and the land—enduring, obdurate and steeped in Aboriginality—has given me some Australianness. Two sources of identification, both spiked with uncertainty, both putting me on the defensive, and yet experienced as intuitively different. But what about the connection between them? Am I condemned always to be the *shleper* of two bags? I return to my books. Arendt's *The Jew as Pariah*, Baumgarten's *City Scriptures*, Alfred Kazin's *New York Jew*. And the fictions: Ozick's novellas, Henry Roth's *Call it Sleep*, Philip Roth's *The Ghost Writer*. I turn then to my own fictions, four novels, each one darker than the last, full of outsiders with frayed and burdensome identities, grappling, often unsuccessfully, with the lack of coherence in their lives. My characters, like so many characters in Jewish fiction, connect their fragmented selves through the imagination, through music and literature in particular.

'It is art that *makes* life' Henry James wrote, it is art that gives life its shape and coherence. For the fiction writer, passionate about art but dispassionate in its creation, the self must be both fluid and fragmented; if it is not, the fiction will be imprisoned forever in autobiography. The process of writing fiction is fraught with uncertainty. Novelists start with little more than an idea and a new ream of paper; they sit at their desks for a couple of years and attempt to write something into existence. It is making sense, coherence, out of unconnected fragments—memories, ideas, events both real and imagined. The writer excavates his/her world in the creation of the characters, but as the fictional world emerges, a certain reciprocity is established: a writer knows more, understands more at the end of a book than at the beginning. And it is this new understanding that so often points the writer in the direction of the next novel. Whether Australian Jew, Aboriginal Australian, Vietnamese Australian, intellectual Australian, fiction provides the means to explore the schisms that exist in all of us who are not of the mainstream.

The 'worldlessness' of the Jew about which Arendt writes so persuasively has drawn the Jew to the arena of the imagination, so perhaps my being a novelist is no more than the dominance of the Jew in my identity equation. I look again at my work. I see the Jew in the ideas, but the contexts are Australian, as are the characters—albeit uneasily. I do not write autobiography, but what I do write provides connections between my own disparate parts. I write fiction to close the gap. I create people with fractured identities, I give them imagination to make life more cogent, more bearable, and in doing so a conduit forms between my own Australian and Jewish parts.

Samovar

Ramona Koval

Ramona Koval is a writer, broadcaster and journalist who, for the last four years, has presented and produced ABC Radio National's 'Books and Writing', Australia's foremost national literary program covering literary matters in Australia and throughout the world. She writes a regular political column in The Australian *newspaper.*

Her interviews and articles have been published in The Age, Quadrant, Australian Book Review, Meanjin *and elsewhere. She is the author of three books of non-fiction—(*Too Many Walnuts, Heinemann, 1993; One to One, *ABC Books, 1994;* Eating Your Heart Out, *Penguin 1986) and a novel,* Samovar, *(Minerva) 1996.*

She has judged the Victorian Premier's Literary Award for non-fiction in 1996, and in 1997 was the Chair of the Committee. She was a judge in the 1997 Walkley Awards for Journalism in the Radio category. She won the 1995 Order of Australia Media Award.

She is the mother of two brilliant daughters.

MOTHER, YOU ARE sitting by the desk as I write. Your hair is twisted into a chignon that you learned from the hairdresser in Paris. He told you that you must suffer to be beautiful. You used to tell me this while you brushed the knots from my hair, pulling the curly fringe from my face.

I told you not to hide your strong forehead, with all the brains in it. And I said to sit up straight, to be proud of your breasts. To be proud you were a woman.

Were you proud to be a woman, Mother?

I had you, didn't I? And your sister. My diamonds, I used to call you. A golden diamond and one fiery red. And now your sister has two babies, and your own two are nearly women. Do you tell them to sit up straight?

They used to listen. Now they don't. I'm waiting for a lull in the proceedings, when they realise I have something to say.

You have? What have you learned, my daughter? In these years we have been apart? I'm ready, I'm here listening. The dead, you know, have time for listening and musing... I'll put my feet up and we will begin. See.

21

I can see. How long has it been—nearly fifteen years since we buried you that miserable October day? I was pregnant with the younger girl, and I wore your grey wool dress to the graveside. It was muddy and there were only a few people there—not my father, of course, but a few close friends and your cousin who had been absent over the years since you fell out with him, I don't know why. But he helped carry your coffin... A rabbi who didn't know you, and your first grand-daughter who was just over two. Many years have passed since I was accountable to you, Mother. I am nearly forty.

Ten years younger than I was when I died. Tell me, if you had only ten years to go, my dear, how would you spend this last decade? After all, you have had so many opportunities—an education, jobs and husbands—why so many husbands?

You had one long miserable marriage—is that better? And I remember you saying that you didn't take anyone else's husband, but you borrowed a few. Remember in the hospital when you were getting another blood transfusion—the last one before you decided you couldn't stand it any more—you said that you had borrowed a few husbands. I borrowed a few and married two.

But I had an excuse. Where was your war?

There is no conversation once you play that card, Mother. You know that and I know that. Now. It's a show stopper, a grand finale, with all the elephants and the tigers and the acrobats parading around.

Why are you talking about circuses? It was no entertainment. It was something to live through. To survive.

Yes, alright. I know. I understand.

Nobody knows. How can you understand? Ah…

You sigh. It upsets me. You used to sigh like that when you lit the Friday night candles, and covered your face in prayer. Or when you lay on the couch reading *Time* magazine during the afternoons when we came home from school.

It was many things. The candles always reminded me of home, of my mother, my brother. Time magazine was filled with other cruelties, insanities. Vietnam, Cambodia… What we went through our war for I do not know. What was the purpose? What did we learn?

You had us, didn't you? That's what I used to say when I saw you sad. Here we are—your two shining diamonds. We were the reward. You were pained, even when you were silent. I remember you'd say a few sentences, something from a memory, and you would lapse into a terrible silence; your eyes would mist up, and I felt I had to fill the silence. With a kiss or a joke or something, anything. I tried to understand. That's all we can do as human beings, surely. To imagine the other's pain, their ordeals. I can't live your experience for you. Just as you can't live mine.

Naturally, because I'm dead, stupid.

But you're not at rest yet, are you? I thought perhaps the dead would be…serene. You used to say, 'It will be quiet in the grave,' and yet you're struggling with the flesh and blood, with the marrow of your life. Are you still tired?

I'm struggling with you, my darling. Not with death, not with life.

Why struggle with me then?

Because you need it. You want it. You called me up.

I called you up to talk, I hope. We are nearly the same age now—we can be frank, we can be friends. See how I'm sitting up straight here—proudly as a woman. We can meet, woman to woman. Why don't I make us a cup of tea?

A long vermouth and dry with a slice of orange at the top would be better. But cut the orange thinly please, not like a peasant.

I'll do my best. But listen Mother, let me tell you what happened this morning. Your grand-daughter, my fourteen-year-old, came to me at four in the morning. She came to my bed because she was worried about her school camp. She couldn't sleep. She's going for two months and she didn't know if she'd like the kids sharing her house. Do you know what I said? I said, 'Your grandmother was four-teen in the war, totally alone. She walked to Warsaw and survived as a Christian. And you're simply going to a school camp for eight weeks!' I actually said that, I can hardly believe my harshness. I mirrored you. Your words out of my mouth. Can the dead speak for the living; what do you think, Mother?

*

The dirt road curves over the hill and sweeps down towards the river, over the misty footbridge and along the valley. A truck comes over the ridge, its headlamps still on, the driver squinting in the first light of day. He grips the wheel with his huge hands as the truck thumps over the potholes, its load moving left and then right, straining on the ropes.

The girl darts behind a clump of trees as she hears the engine approach, slipping down to the mossy base of one, leaning, breathing quickly. She has not rested since she set off in the dark. She opens the small suitcase and takes a crust from the parcel that Mama has given her, chews but cannot taste it. When the truck passes, she stands, straightens the brown wool coat, folds the maroon scarf deep into her singlet, and pulls the kerchief high over her fair plaits tied over her head. She relaces the high black boots.

Mama had cleaned them for her, set them out by the fire with her clothes and the parcel of food. She had been shaken awake in the dark, dressed quickly and walked to the edge of the ghetto wall. 'This is something to remember me by,' her brother said as he took the maroon scarf from under his coat and placed it around her neck. Mama didn't listen to her wails. Mama said to set off, to walk to her new life.

She felt for the leather thong that hung around her neck, suspending the purse that lay there. Inside were the two rings, one gold and one with a blue stone, and the address that Mama had written. This was her only link to her new life, a business partner of her grandfather, a man who would take the rings and give her false papers. 'You must dream of the life that this person had before she was you,' said Mama. 'Your life will depend on this dream.'

She finds the side of the road and begins again. Step, step, step. She huddles in her gait, head down, watching the boots take her to Warsaw. They are muddy now. Good earth, she heard her grandfather's voice in her ear, gives rise to good crops. She had driven down this road riding high in his carved cart, the four horses dancing, making light work. He let her hold the reins as he sung his prayers. His red and white beard was long, and the wind sent it over each shoulder.

She slows a little as she checks the rings again. She pulls the leather thong from between her breasts, and opens the purse. One ring, two rings, and the address. She closes the purse and places it back. She trips on a stone, but doesn't fall.

Mama came to Warsaw; sometimes she stayed for one month or two. She and Yankel would cry, since their father had died soon after her birth, and they were attached to their Mama, but Grandfather whispered, 'She's still young, not thirty yet; she is entitled to a life.'

Near the river, the fog is thick, she can see no more than ten steps ahead. She thinks of the false papers, and wonders who she will be. An aristocrat, a shopgirl, a ballerina—Anna Pavlova. As she climbs the ridge the fog lifts and the sun is red and low. Three days to Warsaw lie ahead of her, days without papers, without the yellow star on her coat. She must be invisible.

The cows hardly look up as she hurries past them. She can hear them tearing the grass, and chewing it slowly. It is light now, and she paces herself with the cows, not the race of her heart.

*

You can imagine how I felt, can't you, sending my only daughter away. At fourteen.

So this is my grandmother?

It is. Your grandmother Leah. I kept the children together for three years in the ghetto—three years with my mother who was sick too. Typhus. The bodies of the dead in the streets. Do you know how hard it was to keep clean, to nurse people in such a situation? What could I do? There were all sorts of rumours—liquidation. I was a widow with a sick mother and two beautiful children. My son was growing, sixteen and dark. Black eyes and dark, dark hair. And my daughter. A beauty with her father's blue eyes and blond hair. She looked like them. She could pass for one of them. She was the only one of us who might get through. What could I do? Sentence her to death like the rest of us?

I thought you didn't love me. I thought you wanted my brother with you because he was your favourite. I was totally alone. I wanted to go back with you. I was afraid... See how this room is getting crowded. I am called up by my daughter, I call my own mother up from the silence.

She looks just like me, Mother. Grandmother and I could be twins. How old is she?

Let me think. She had me when she was twenty-two, she died when I was seventeen. So she's thirty-nine—exactly your age. She was shot with her son and her mother. Just before the war ended. She kept her son and her mother alive and then they were betrayed. Someone told the Germans where they were hiding. I walked back to my town as the war was ending. I went to the town and found the horse with one ear. And looked for the hunchbacked peasant who was hiding them. He was dead. Someone told me the story. The Germans threw a torch into the deep cellar. The flames leapt. My mother ran out first, and then my brother. He was carrying his grandmother over his shoulder. He was eighteen. They shot him first and then the others.

Oh, Mother.

For the whole war I saw my mother and my brother in my mind's eye. I imagined my brother being comforted by her. He was the apple of her eye. We had no father. He was the only boy. He was quiet and responsible. He carried things. He did the heavier work. He climbed up on ladders. He was our man. I longed for them. I saw my grandmother baking and my mother sewing. She stayed with them and didn't go to Warsaw any more. And then, when it was all over, then, nothing. They were gone. I fainted, and when I woke up I was in a convent hospital and the war was over. It had been over for two months.

*

One step after another. Now crossing the bridge, cold grey stones, over the river. The footpath is shared with workers hurrying in the crisp dawn. Army transports exhale their diesel fumes. She holds the leather case tightly in her gloved hand, the other clutches her coat tightly around her. The dusty road has changed to cobblestones, and she sees the danger in people observing the mud on her boots. There is no mud in Warsaw. They might know that she is a girl from the country. What is she doing here? Who is she?

Slipping along an alley she finds a doorway and sits: she spits in her handkerchief and wipes away the mud. She pulls at the caked soil with her fingernails. Spits and spits again. She is parched, so her spittle is dry. She must wipe away the mud—transformation, obliteration, quickly, quickly, before anyone sees. What if someone is watching her? What if they come and take her rings? What if they turn her into the police? Spit, spit.

When they are dully clean, she stands, adjusts her kerchief, and takes out the address. Ogrodowa Street, number seventeen. How will she find it? She must ask someone. They might hear her accent, she might sound Jewish. The Yiddish they spoke at home—the *mammaloshen*, the mother tongue—stuck in her throat. Mother tongue. Mother cast her out. It must never pass her lips again. She thought of Madame Krinsky, the teacher at her school. She was from Warsaw. She spoke like a lady. She whispered some words in the way that Madame Krinsky would have spoken.

'Excuse me, Sir, I am looking for Ogrodowa Street. Can you possibly direct me there?' 'Excuse me, Sir. I seem to have lost my way. I was looking for Ogrodowa Street. How silly of me—could you show me how to get back there?'

Madame Krinsky patted her hair and laughed a little laugh. She could never do that.

But Miriam resumes her walk, now with her face raised a little like Madame Krinsky. She had to look as if she belonged on this street, as if she had always lived here. She saw the rubble from the bombings, and the old buildings that were still standing. She had come here with her mother sometimes on shopping trips. These boots that took her to her new life were bought in the big department store where they had an account.

A baker loading up his truck with sweet dark loaves manoeuvres his cart along the path. He is covered in flour, his face pale and his cap well back on his head. She had relatives with a flour factory. Her grandmother used their flour in her bakery. Dough and yeast and pastry ran in the family. His loaves smell good, and she is hungry.

Should she go in? She'll have to speak if she does. Get to the address quickly, get off the streets. You have no papers. You do not exist.

'Excuse me, Sir—can I buy a roll from you? They smell so good, they look so beautiful.'

'These are for the canteen. The army. We don't sell to the public any more.'

'Oh. Please then, could you possibly direct me to Ogrodowa Street? I seem to have lost my way.'

'You're not from around here?'

'No! I'm just a bit lost. I've been sick and I've had trouble remembering things.'

The baker finished loading the cart, and pushed it to the door of the shop. He let the load steady on the step, and he pulled his cap forward.

'Ogrodowa Street is about a dozen blocks over this way. There's a park on the corner.'

'Thank you Sir. Yes I remember the park now.'

He selected two warm golden rolls from the tray on the bench, and wrapped them in newspaper. He gave them to her, putting a finger to his lips.

'Here, take them, and hurry. A girl alone is in great danger here. Find your address and keep indoors. And don't think you can come here again. I have a business to run, and these times are not easy for anybody.'

She put the parcel into her long coat pocket. It warmed her thigh. Her heart beat in her ears. How had he known? She must be more careful. She must not be so stupid. She heard her mother's parting words... 'You must survive so that they will not be able to say that they killed all of us. You must not forget you are Jewish. You must go on to have some children, so we will live in them. Go now.'

She almost forgot her hunger in the panic of imagining the worst. She tore a hole in the top of the parcel, and pulled out a piece of bread. It was good. She remembered how Yankel would take her to the bakery and by the time they got back the loaf would have been hollowed out.

It was fully light now, and the city was alive. People walked faster here; was it just that they ambled at home, or was it the pace of war? She counted the street blocks: six, seven, eight, nine, ten. What should she say when she came to number seventeen Ogrodowa Street? Her mother said that these people would help her. They were business associates of her grandfather, Polish business people.

She came to the door of number seventeen in a long wide street lined with trees. The house was three storeys high, of stately grey stone, two hundred years old. 'Elegant' would be her mother's term for it. The heavy knocker rang through the lower storey.

A small plump women opened the door, her apron tied around her several times like a hospital nurse, and she narrowed her dark eyes.

'I'm here to see Mr Podlaska, he is expecting me.'

The woman tightened her lips over her teeth.

'Come in quickly, and wipe your feet. I've just polished the floor. Wait in here.'

Miriam stood by the door of the marble entrance hall, and she uncovered her hair. The kerchief was damp with the morning dew and she stuffed it into the pocket. The other roll was still there, and she calculated how long it would last. Two days in the ghetto. And she had eaten one whole roll in the last fifteen minutes. She must be more careful.

The clock in the hall ticked steadily—and she thought of the clock in her grandfather's house. Zeida Enoch was almost as tall as his clock. Once she had hidden in there to avoid punishment she was due for kicking over a bucket of milk. Whenever Yankel or Miriam transgressed, the whole family felt it could scold, to make up for the lack of a father. Many smacks instead of one. She hid in the clock until the hour, until she was so frightened by the sound that she cried out.

The door behind the stairs opened and a man came out.

'Are you Miriam, Stotski's grand-daughter?'

'Yes, Sir.'

'Have you got something for me?'

'Yes, Sir,' and she pulled the purse by the thong,

opened it with trembling fingers, and handed him the rings.

'Good, come with me.'

He led her down the back stairs to the cellar, a large cold room with pipes and a coal heater, and behind this room, another, in which stood a bed, a bucket, a bookshelf and a dog kennel.

'Now listen to me carefully. I am going to take a photograph of you, to put on the papers I have arranged. You are no longer Miriam, grand-daughter of Stotski. Your name is Halina Kowakowska. She is twenty-one years old. How old are you?'

'Fourteen.'

'Well, Halina, you are going to have to become older, fast. You'll have to put up your braids and walk like a woman, not a girl.'

'Who is she, Halina?'

'Halina flew out of here last week to join her family in London. She is there, and you are here, and now, you are her. You will stay in the cellar until you are no longer safe. You are to look after our dog Rolf, and we expect you to clean for us and work in the house. In return we'll feed you and let you stay. I warn you that my son-in-law is a journalist and he is worried that he will be watched. He lives with my daughter on the top storey. He didn't want you to come here, he didn't know Stotski like I did. I beg you to stay in the cellar when he is at home, never go outside during the day, and if you need to walk, take Rolf for a walk at night. Now you can sleep and Jadwiga will bring you some soup. Then you will meet Rolf.'

'Thank you Sir. And my grandfather would thank you for your kindness.'

He left the room and climbed the metal staircase to the ground floor. When the door shut behind him the only glow in the cellar was a bare electric bulb. Miriam breathed and lay on the bed. The scratchy blanket was sharp against her face, and she closed her eyes. She thought of the high feather pillows at home, and the starched white pillowcases. She must not cry. She must not make a sound. She was Halina Kowakowska, the daughter of a good Polish family and she was twenty-one years old. She kissed her childhood goodbye.

*

Mother, I'm writing your story as you hoped I would, but it's so hard, there are so many gaps. I have no idea of the real sequence of events. I have snapshots. Four photographs that I saw as a child. I've lost two of them since you died. The first one is of you and Yankel in the ghetto just before you left. He is standing with his arm around you and you have your hand in the pocket of your coat.

See that yellow armband with the Star of David? Yankel hated it, and he put his arm around me to protect his dignity. He was ashamed of being marked like the cattle. He looked after me. He didn't want me to go, but he didn't want me to stay.

The second photograph is the one they took of you as Halina, for your identity papers. Your fair braids are across the top of your head. You are smiling, but your eyes are blank.

*A proper little German maiden, hey? A fräulein I was. I had a
good ear for languages, I learned to speak German without even
a hint of Yiddish, and I spoke Polish like a princess. I was a
devout Catholic. I prayed and prayed till my knees hurt on the
stone. I prayed to Jesus, Mary, anybody that might hear. Did it
help?*

The third picture is of you walking arm in arm down a
wide pavement in Warsaw with a young man. He is wearing a suit, a hat, and walks with confidence. You have both
extended your right legs forward, as if you are walking in
formation. Yet you have that same frozen smile. And
hollow eyes. You are wearing high heels.

*I was sixteen by then, he was my boyfriend, you could say. He
took me to my first opera.* Tristan and Isolde. *I was so mes-
merised by the audience of German officers and Polish
collaborators that I could hardly hear the music. He was very
polite, he bought me coffee and even chocolate. His father was a
big man with a monocle. The musical director, a Wagnerian!
And there I was sitting next to him, hardly daring to breathe.*

Did you sleep with your boyfriend?

*Don't be so stupid. Why talk about sex or romance? It was a
war and I was trying to survive.*

But you can talk about this now. I am older and you have
been dead for fifteen years. We can talk like women. You
once said that throughout the war you did nothing that you
were ashamed of. That you were not a prostitute and that
you didn't steal food from others' mouths. That, I accept,

Mother. But I'm talking here of comfort and warmth and a sense of oblivion. That would be understandable.

Listen you. Halina Kowakowska went to church on Sunday mornings and again in the evenings. She was from a good family. Boys like Heniek didn't take sluts to the opera. Are you an idiot? With all your education, why don't you think properly. What a waste of brains!

The fourth photograph is taken from the street. It looks up to a third-storey window, and you are looking down. You are trying to do the smile, trying to make the face light up, but you look defeated, pasty, battered. It's a wooden house, a plain facing, a barracks.

That was in Warsaw. Just before the ghetto uprising. I was working in a munitions factory, making explosives. We were all sick from the yellow powder, it got on our skin, in our finger-nails, in our eyes. We tasted it with our food. We spat out yellow globs in the morning. I was so, so tired. The girls there would listen to the shooting from the ghetto. 'The Jews are fighting back,' they would say. 'They are fighting the Germans!'

I was sharing a room with two others. They were lesbians and I could hear them making love in the night. I used to pull the blanket up over my ears not to hear them. Sometimes they would bring men in for the money. I would lie in my bunk, pretending to be asleep, hoping to die.

Just after those girls took the photograph I put on my boots and my coat—it was a Sunday morning I remember, and I was on my way to church. And I passed by the gates of the ghetto and I heard more gunshots, and I decided that I had had enough.

I was tired of being Halina. I was afraid even while I slept of saying something, saying a word of Yiddish, giving myself away.

So I found myself walking up to the guard. A fine tall blond German soldier with pale blue eyes. 'Let me in, I belong here, I want to go in.' This is what I said to him!

'Don't be mad, young woman, this place is only for Jews. It's going to be cleared soon. It's not a place for you.'

I begged him again. But he told me to go and pushed me away with his rifle butt. There was no place for me anywhere. I stood there, alone, and invisible, finally.

Breitbart, the Strongest Jew

Bernard Cohen

Bernard Cohen is the author of Tourism *(1992),* The Blindman's Hat *(1997), which won the 1996* Australian/Vogel Literary Award *and* Snowdome *(1998). His short fiction, essays and reviews have appeared in newspapers, magazines and literary journals in Australia, New Zealand, France and the United States.*

He is currently completing a story collection, 'Hardly Beach Weather', and is also writing 'The Antibiography of Robert Fucking Menzies'.

Bernard Cohen lives in the Blue Mountains west of Sydney, and can also be found at http://www.hermes.net.au/bernard/

I AM BREITBART, THE strongest Jew in Galicia, the strongest in the world, and when I flex these bony, ridiculous arms, I can bend a horseshoe. I can tie it in a knot. Biceps like boulders, elbows for shoulders, legs as toned as the courthouse columns. When I stretch my arms upward, it makes not a gnat of difference whether they lift an anvil or press the pungent air.

But don't worry yourselves if you hear fearsome tales of my terrible deeds. 'Heart of gold' is also me: so says my sister explaining the accident with the rock and the window. I'm muscly as a ferryman, but still soft inside, soft as the torn centre of a loaf which, believe me, I appreciate eating. And I'm young enough to sip the strawberry wine, innocent as anything, straight out of my father's glass, and feel the dizziness my parents' guests take hours to accumulate.

My big sister laughs because she thinks I'm under control. She thinks that I'm cute as a rich man's pony. On the contrary, I'm stringy and tough as the neighbour's goat. At the *Shabbes* meal, we see that the soil is softened by the grass which is softened by the innumerable stomachs of a cow, whose meat distils all that has gone to feed it. This is wonderful, and proof that the world is divine. With that I have no trouble agreeing. But you should know this: I'm tough enough to eat the unprocessed dirt. No pastry wrapping for my mudpies, folks, no bread and butter to diminish the fulsome earthy taste. I'm Breitbart and—though, as I said, I'm not about to eat up your house—if I were so inclined, I'd chew my way through to Australia.

I'm five years old and daring as a Maccabee. I'm so powerful, the evening sun stands still in the sky that I might play under the fruit trees for ten extra minutes while my mother calls, 'Shmuel, Shmulik! Come and eat! You want me to cook the soup dry?'

Of course I don't, but there are times when a young muscleman must prepare himself for the forthcoming day, a day when Breitbart himself—no dwarfish imitation, this one—comes to Horodenka.

Tomorrow in the marketplace I will see Breitbart lift a cow above his head and hold it there while the crowd shouts in unison: 'One! Two! Three! Four!' and the cow trying to kick, trying to figure out about gravity now the earth has been so assertively displaced, trying to bellow, 'Put me down, you cheeky little urchin.'

'Five! Six!' call the men, as Breitbart puffs out his cheeks like a trombonist, and all the vermilion sunsets of Europe take place on his forehead.

'Seven! Eight! Nine!' as the cow gives up the struggle and—cattle having shorter memories than people—forgets that she ever walked on the ground.

'Ten!' and the whole village cheers because Breitbart is still the strongest Jew who can not only pick up a cow and hold it in the air for Ten, he can put it back down gently. Breitbart regains his pallor and the cow gingerly steps towards a patch of long grass.

I will lift a cow in each hand, pressing them upwards so they sag somewhat and their four legs make a cube, and while I hold the cows up in the air like this and the village cheers, I will dance a cow-holding jig. I will do this now and Breitbart will see what I can do—and me a five-year-old child!—and will say, 'Oy! Little boy, you must come travel the country with me. Together we will lift the heaviest carriages. Together we will be the strongest and—if they will speculate...no, no 'ifs'...they *will* speculate, endlessly—no one will be sure which of us is the master and which the apprentice.'

Rivka, my sister, overhears. Her eyes momentarily hold a meniscus of tears then overflow. I'm going, she knows, but she doesn't say, 'Don't go, little brother. Don't go my Shmoo.' She is silent.

And though I too am crying—and not ashamed to admit it to the entire village, for my sister is the best friend imaginable for ever and ever—though I am crying, I know I must go with Breitbart. My sister and I embrace in silence: we will not see each other until our childhoods are gone.

*

In the future when the first cellar is full of drunken soldiers shouting and asking my father, 'Where are your daughters?' and laughing, we are hidden in the second cellar behind the sliding panel which my father installed for just this event, for such a happening as this. In the future when I am no longer five years old—five and already I know how not to cry though in the dark, in the dusty

43

dark—and when something brushes against my leg in the dust of the second cellar, when we are there, I will be Breitbart's best-ever apprentice with the strength to hold shut the door of the second cellar against the 'What's this?' of the soldiers, and if the panel appeared to give a little at the soldier's first push, it doesn't budge further and the soldier thinks he must have imagined it and proceeds with his drinking and asking my father, 'What vintage?' and laughing until all the soldiers are calling out the names of years and my father is pretending to laugh along with them; and when he offers them two jars for their journey one says, 'Yes, we will' and another says, 'Thank you'—more polite than he's ever been to a Jew, most probably, as my father says later when we have come out into the day and he can boast quietly, and my sister and I can admire his courage.

In the future when the borders of nations try to intervene between a boy at school and his family at home, when the boy has been sent to a larger town to continue his education and the borders try to cut the old nation in two and cleave each part to another nation, and I am stuck in the large town though it's the middle of summer and the school has closed and everyone else has gone home and I sleep on the schoolmaster's sister's kitchen floor on a thin mat: when I see this future approaching I will grit my teeth and grip the border in my strong fingers and wrestle it like Samson tearing at the pillars—like Breitbart stilling a bull—and fight that wriggling boundary right back to where it was. And my father will come to collect me, not noticing that anything could have been amiss, never noticing that his son's fingers are black with rubbed-off ink and that the streets are smeared with the disturbed ink from the worn marks on the map too.

In the future, further again, virtually unforeseeable, there will be a banner in Horodenka which reads 'The Two Breitbarts', and the entire village will turn out to watch us bend and straighten lamp posts, juggle sheep and lift carts clear into the air. My mother and father will be in the crowd, so happy, so much *naches* I have brought to them, and they will be whispering to each other, 'But he was so thin as a child, so thin.'

But is he Jewish?

Elisabeth Wynhausen

Elisabeth Wynhausen was born in the Netherlands and grew up in Sydney. A journalist who has worked for many newspapers and magazines, she is a senior writer on The Australian. *This extract is from her memoir,* Manly Girls.

WE CAME TO AUSTRALIA by accident. My aunt Ali, the bookworm, read *A Town Like Alice* and convinced the others that Australia was a land of opportunity. With little idea of what to expect, my aunts and uncles shipped the furniture, the Frigidaire and the wash basins to the unknown continent, and went on ahead, quickly writing to say that it never rained in Sydney. Having given away our raincoats, we took off on the long flight.

Delayed by engine trouble in Darwin, where the temperature was about 40°C, passengers waited all day in the airport, a tin shed in a field of dust. Faintly discouraged, we flew to Sydney. Our arrival, in the second week of January 1951, was recorded for posterity. Uncle Nick, a gregarious man uninhibited by his halting English, had convinced the photographer from the *Sydney Morning Herald* that we were people of some note, and as we stepped onto the tarmac, exhausted, crumpled and irritated, with my three-year-old brother Jules in tears from the shock of landing, the photographer sprang forward and took our picture.

The rain began the following afternoon and kept up for three weeks.

The country town of Maitland, north of Sydney, was flooded. The newspapers had front-page pictures of the disaster. People were being rescued by rowboat from the roofs of outlying buildings and livestock had to be left to drown. Though the Dutch are famous for making polders out of marshland, and draining fields that would otherwise lie under water, my parents were peculiarly disconcerted by the idea of what had happened around Maitland. *A Town Like Alice* had prepared them for almost any climatic oddity, but not, of all things, a flood. Reminded that they knew nothing about the land, they decided to stay in Sydney, for the time being.

Before the end of 1951 they, together with Bram and Ali, had bought a house in Lewis Street, Balgowlah, a staid, peninsular suburb between the Spit Bridge and the road to the northern beaches. People of means insisted on calling it Balgowlah Heights and, with suburbia starting to take itself seriously, they prevailed.

Our own unenviable position did not inhibit the local responses to us, however, and we were welcomed as the first foreigners to move into the neighbourhood. Up at the local shops, people my mother half-recognised might work a conversation around to the point where they could re-assure her that we were a good type of migrant.

*

By the time I was eleven or twelve years old, I was aware that something was missing from the domestic arrange-ments that the locals made, but I was intrigued by the way that they lived, and going next door to watch television had some of the enchantment of a long journey. In the Turners' house the rooms were small, the windows were small, and papery Holland blinds the colour of parchment were drawn at all times in all seasons. Usually, of an evening, Mrs T. did not leave the kitchen and her husband was hardly to be seen at all. If the two of them were at war they did not speak to each other, and although this called for a degree of self-restraint unimaginable in our household, they hardly seemed to notice it as anything out of the ordinary. My brother and I were asked to stay regardless of the conflict.

The neighbours' tea seemed to be the only thing they had agreed on when they were married. It was a mixed grill with a pork sausage, a small lamb chop, a rasher of bacon, half a grilled tomato, a puddle of peas and a scoop of mashed potato. The unchanging nature of the meal never failed to surprise me; nor did the occasion itself, because Tom Turner and his little sister were left to their own devices at dinner and, in spite of the arrangement of the furniture (the chairs lined up on either side of the sofa, so everyone could sit in the front stalls), we sat cross-legged on the living room floor, with our plates in our laps, the lights switched off and the telly turned up loud. In our house, in contrast, the only excuse for being left alone was that you had homework, or a headache, conversations went on uninterrupted between two rooms and everyone had to report in for meals around the kitchen table.

We were drawn to the kitchen, in any case, but it was difficult to imagine that happening in an Australian household, judging by the people that I visited after school. The kitchens were most unfamiliar. If there was any food, it was hidden away in high cupboards: biscuit tins were out of reach; instead of fruit there were wax bananas on a cut-glass epergne, and the canisters in mint condition had obviously been squared away with a ruler.

In public, parents and children acted as if they hardly knew each other and they weren't much different in private. If they kissed at all, they kissed like people worried about giving each other the 'flu. It did not surprise me that my pals couldn't wait to get away from home, but I, for the most part, could not wait to get away from school.

The first day at Harbord Primary had started with a misunderstanding. Mrs Kelsick, the fourth class teacher, had made a speech. The general drift of it was that I was a New Girl who had only just got to lovely Australia. 'Of course we'll do our best to make her feel at home, won't we girls,' she said. Occupied in trying not to take the giggling at the back of the room personally, I waited to correct her until the others had gone out for playlunch. 'Yes, dear,' she said patiently, 'of course you feel at home here.'

The first impression died hard. Although I spoke in a broad Australian accent at school, Mrs Kelsick remained convinced that I was just off the boat, and if she marvelled over my spelling the class was reminded that it was being shown up by a New Australian. I would vow to lose the spelling bee next time but I couldn't help myself, and Mrs Kelsick did not seem to know, as yet, that ex-wogs were always the best spellers, something I had found out at the primary school in Balgowlah Heights, where Jules, cousin Ron and I took line honours until a skinny kid from Yugoslavia turned up and got 'aquarium' right the first time.

*

Not long ago, someone who took us under his wing when we moved to Lewis Street, Balgowlah, told my mother he hadn't known that we were Jewish. 'How is that possible?' she asked him, as if he had wilfully refused to acknowledge the obvious. It wasn't the sort of thing you had to tell the neighbours in Europe, and my guess is that she never really understood what it meant to have settled in a part of Sydney where Jews existed only in theory. Things may have been different in Coogee, in the eastern suburbs, where whole streets suddenly seemed to fill with what the *Bulletin* called 'the brooding aliens' from the DP camps, and the kindest local interpretation was that a Jew was a generic reffo, lost property without a rightful destination. Out our way, though, there was no reason to associate my mother's determined gaiety with what was, strictly speaking, a figure of speech: even if Jews crept in the conversational back door as pawnbrokers or were people who stiffed you in a financial transaction, why would they suddenly materialise out of thin air to park those bloody trucks and vans across the street?

Even someone who knew a thing or two about the Jews could have been confused by our behaviour, particularly at Christmas, which we overdid a bit the first time around, delivering more presents than the Smith Family, too excited to notice the embarrassed pause before someone's mum told us to come back later because they still had to wrap the gifts for us. The only way we could possibly have drawn attention to ourselves was in our eagerness to conform, but my mother appears to have forgotten the degree of her discretion in those days, when we were trying to fit in without people making too much of a fuss.

By no means all the Jews who fled from Europe were in a hurry to flaunt the pedigree. Sydney seemed to be a haven, but who could be sure? The Jews of Amsterdam had felt more or less secure for centuries and, in the years before the war, were inclined to brag about their assimilation, going so far as to contrast it with the 'primitive' way of life in the shtetls of Eastern Europe.

It made very little difference in the end. More than three-quarters of the Jews in Holland were murdered by the Nazis. My mother's mother, Elisabeth Nathans, was gassed at Sobibor, a death camp on the eastern border of Poland. My father's father, Jules Wynhausen, was deported, and only this year I found out that he also died in Sobibor.

Neither my brother nor I were able to confront the manner of their going. We were aware that our grandparents had died during the war, but we never asked questions about it, as if frightened of straying into a territory that had been sealed off for good. Nevertheless, those unexplained deaths assumed an odd, almost sacred character, as if in talking about them we would dissipate the sense of significance that was the mainspring of our identity as Jews.

*

The Netherlands capitulated on May 15, 1940, a day after the bombardment of Rotterdam, and five days after the German army marched across the border. Anti-Jewish regulations were posted frequently. When my mother's brother, Bram, married Ali, the family had to troop into the town hall in Arnhem to apply and pay for permits to travel by train to the wedding in the north. Jewish homes were raided by night and people were taken away to 'work camps'. By the spring of 1942, several of the Nathans cousins had been deported and the family tried, to little avail, to keep the news from my grandfather, who was gravely ill because he could not get medicine for his heart condition.

After his death, a month later, they went into hiding, or spirited themselves out of Arnhem, with little more than the clothes they were wearing. My mother carried a small basket with a skirt, a blouse, a comb, a brush and a mirror. She did not have false papers. Nor did her companions, her brother Nico, and his friend, Dolf. They slipped over the frontier, spent the night half-asleep in a hayrick, brushed off as best they could—the sort of detail mum would never leave out of a story—and caught a bus to Antwerp.

To pass for local people visiting relatives, they edged from one town to the next, but that did not make them any less conspicuous when they cut across a field at first light; almost as soon as they were over the border, they were picked up by a couple of German soldiers. My mother, who spoke fluent French, was interviewed that afternoon by the local captain of the gendarmes, and on the spur of the moment confided to him that she had been involved with the Underground, helping French prisoners of war who had escaped. That was reason enough for her to have been handed straight over to the Nazis, but she had guessed right: the policeman said that he would leave the cells unlocked, and told her where to hide with Nico and Dolf while the search was carried out.

It all went according to plan: they were aboard the train in Lille the following morning, when a stranger wandering along the platform stopped by the window and tossed in a bunch of violets, with the compliments of the captain. 'Violets,' I marvelled as a child, because violets were her favourite, and my mother smiled a bit complacently, not above revelling in the gallantry of the gesture which capped her story.

In almost any situation, she can find an incident to suggest that things were not as bad as you might have imagined, but nothing lightens the memory of the longest night of her life, the night that they waited on the demarcation line to dodge into unoccupied France. Someone in the Resistance had led them to a place at the river's edge, under a bridge patrolled by soldiers with dogs that barked at every sound. Too frightened even to whisper, they lay dead-still in the reeds, with big water snails crawling over them. 'Think what we've come through,' my mother told herself, and thought instead about Arnhem, where her mother had stayed behind. 'Think about tomorrow...' She was feverish, with a severely infected throat, and could not stop shivering. But when the patrol changed at dawn the three of them waded across the river, so keyed up, all of a sudden, that they kept going for another five kilometres before they hung their clothes on the bushes to dry.

An acquaintance in the Resistance in Lyons talked them out of going on to Spain, instead advising my mother and her companions to try to slip into Switzerland.

Up in the mountains of the Haute Savoie, they walked about sixteen hours, going by mountainous backroads, to the high barbed wire at the border. The men struggled through, and Nico held the strands of wire together for his sister. When he let it go, the snap of the wire echoed like a rifle shot, and in less than a minute the guard from the Swiss frontier post was after them.

Though they had agreed to scatter, if it came to that, meeting up again at a particular place in Berne, gallant Dolf stayed with my mother, only to be arrested as well. From the frontier post, the two of them were driven to the police station at Geneva in a Black Maria. Somehow it still makes my mother laugh. Though the cold-hearted Swiss put countless refugees straight back across the border—in effect handing some of them over to the Nazis—the policeman who interviewed my mother in Geneva promised to let her brother stay, if she revealed his whereabouts. To his astonishment Nico was not only picked up, in Berne, but sentenced to three weeks in gaol, on the official charge of deserting his sister. 'Well, it could have been worse,' mum would say, shamelessly. The policeman who had interviewed her seemed to have his hopes. Nothing came of it, but meanwhile, she was shown around Geneva in a police car.

Neither Jules nor I used to ask our parents questions about the war. If they had a drink or two, and reminisced, we listened in silence, aware of the fragile mood of the occasion, unwilling to get in over our heads. It was as if we did not want to know too much, sensing the desolation that the stories covered up. We drew back even further than they did, and they talked about their war as if, against the odds, they had often managed to have a high old time.

*

It did not occur to me for a long time that the sense of unease that I stifled as a child (or circumvented, by misbehaving instead of trying to fit in) was related to what my parents had failed to say about being Jewish. The question was not so much ignored, as shelved. Of course I knew what I was meant to do: I was neither to conceal my Jewishness nor to make a show of it, as if being a Jew was a bit like wearing clean underwear every day; you knew it was there (in case of a traffic accident), but you did not have to tell the world about it.

I found out later that other children were given a series of warnings before they went out amongst Gentiles; even a birthday party was fraught with danger, because a Jewish kid could blacken the name of the whole race by accidentally taking the biggest piece of cake on the plate. Luckily no-one had said anything like that to me. I was an insistently noisy child always trying to claim the centre of attention, and at home I fitted right in. At family parties with the uncles present, they all competed for attention, shouted to be heard and argued for the sake of argument. They debated angrily over trifles, disagreeing at full volume, for instance, about the merits of a particular brand of petrol. Unobservant in our turn, we children failed to notice that other grown-ups shouted in private, not in front of witnesses.

It didn't occur to me or my relatives that I was noisy and pushy, *just like a Jew*, because I was just like them—an echt Nathans, for whom all social life was a performance, verging on a compulsion. The Nathanses would have been astonished to hear that their behaviour, on occasion, fitted the stereotype. They thought of themselves as originals and they did not doubt that they could bend the rules, a bit.

My mother has never hesitated to adapt the Christian religion to our requirements. Perhaps that was why we did not give a thought to the implications of celebrating Christmas, until we were sprung with a tree and all the trimmings. The tree, a pine, was government property that dad chopped down after dark, hesitating every time that we heard a car approaching. At home, done up with cotton-wool puffs and silver twine, it looked just right, like a photograph in the *Australian Women's Weekly*.

I was tidying it up on Christmas Day when the bell rang unexpectedly and a Dutch couple marched in. Behind them was their daughter Elly who was in my class at Jewish Sunday school. I stayed where I was under the tree, waiting for the earth to swallow me up. Elly, who had not moved either, stood transfixed just inside the loungeroom, staring at the tree as if she had never seen anything like it. 'Oh, I see,' said her father unnecessarily, adjusting his rimless spectacles. Perhaps he sniffed. The turkey was almost done. 'You celebrate Christmas...'

The episode crystallised what I felt about going to Sunday school, and going to Sunday school almost put me off Jews for life. The only synagogue on our side of the harbour was at Lindfield, on the North Shore. The elite—third, even fourth-generation Australians, who took their cues from the *anciens riches* of the district—did not go out of their way to mingle with the likes of us. In fact, the children whose parents were the congregation's movers and shakers were in one class at the Sunday school, and those of us from out our way, or from equally unfashionable suburbs like Hornsby, at the end of the northern line, were in another.

Even the playground had its unofficial demarcation line, and we kept away from the little princesses whose court shoes clicked on the cement. Their propriety was astonishing. Their socks did not fall down, their hair ribbons were never limp, and they wore smocked velvet dresses, the like of which one saw only in shop windows. They knew how to behave, of course, and on the morning that I dropped my prayer book, one of them materialised on the spot, to remind me in a penetrating whisper to kiss the book, in penitence.

My brother and I never failed to protest, but every Sunday, for three years, we were transported the twelve miles to Lindfield, to scratch away in a language that seemed as dusty as the Dead Sea Scrolls.

*

My mother was startled into action the first time that a boy asked me out. His name was Brian, he was at least an inch and a half taller than I, and we met after the foxtrot in my school's assembly hall. Indicating a preference which made me think that there must be something wrong with him, Brian sidled over to ask if he could have the pleasure of 'this, er...'. After he telephoned the next day, my mother stopped just short of the Torquemada in her efforts to find out about him, but restrained herself from asking if he were Jewish. The question was redundant. He lived in Frenchs Forest, where there are about as many Jews as there are in Mecca.

It took me only three days to get ready to go to the Balgowlah Odeon with him. I thought of it as a historic occasion. Every other fifteen-year-old in the universe had been putting theory into practice for years, while I sat at home, reading *Seventeen* magazine's advice about how to act on the first date, though all I needed to know, in the event, was how you explained to a boy who had only just managed to inch his arm across your shoulders that your parents insisted on picking you up outside the cinema.

Less than a month later, Jules and I were packed off to summer camp, almost without warning. 'You always liked going to camp,' mum said triumphantly. The camp had some connection with a youth movement called Betar, but further inquiries were fruitless—it was not in my mother's nature to accumulate extraneous information, and she knew everything about Betar that she needed to know. 'What's to ask,' she said, and went on dusting down the suitcases, 'it's a Jewish camp.'

The Betar people were waiting around out the back of Sydney's Central Railway by Eddy Avenue. They wore navy blue shirts with a white lanyard, and a cap—just like the WRAAFs had in the second world war—tucked into the shoulder tab. No-one appeared to have warned them against advertising that they were Jewish, because they shrieked '*shalom, shalom*' if anyone they knew turned up. Jules nudged me, grinning. Several of them were swearing loudly enough for all the world to hear, the first hint that we were to find the campers to our liking. Startling as it was to find out that we had anything in common with other Jews, we very soon felt as if we had known them all along, and within a day or two my brother and I unselfconsciously

declared ourselves to be Betarim. The camp site just outside Sutherland on the southern edge of Sydney was owned
by an obscure Christian fellowship.

We were being toughened up with bush walks and
Camp Pie only for the time that we would desert Australia
to go to Israel. Betar existed to transform namby-pamby
Jewish youth into Zionist warriors, but first, in the words
of its dated inspirational material, we had to abandon 'the
slovenly habits of the suppressed ghetto Jew'. On the banks
of the Woronora River, outside Sutherland, this appeared
to mean that one was betraying one's revised heritage by
fighting with Ruthie Goldberg about whose turn it was to
wash up.

We were taught a supposed self-defence technique. In
the process of becoming what the founder of Betar had
called 'the new type of Jew', we spent hours flailing away
at one another with sticks. No-one bothered to explain
how stick-fighting, a loosely-adapted martial art, was going
to help the new type of Jew in a border dispute with the
old type of Arab, but that did not haunt the likes of us. We
were the heirs to a militant tradition.

Betar's propaganda traced a direct line of succession
from the martyrs of Masada—who had killed themselves
instead of being captured by the Romans—to the Irgun
Zvai Leumi, one of three underground organisations operating in Palestine at the time of the British Mandate. Betar
had been the breeding ground of some of the terrorists in
the Irgun, who bombed the King David Hotel in
Jerusalem, military headquarters of the British, in one of
the bloodier moments of the campaign to dislodge them.

The first reffos from the D.P. camps were then sailing

towards Australia, and their arrival was not universally welcomed. Newspaper headlines referred to a 'rush of Jews'; rabid politicians said that Australia should not be a 'dumping ground' for what the official racists called 'the refuse of Europe'; and the *Bulletin*, drawing a long bow, linked all Jews to the terrorists in Palestine.

Betar had started in Sydney that year. The sense of timing alone was enough to hint at its posture, and though the situation had changed by 1961, the message had not. Betar was as belligerent as ever.

All in all, it may not have been the summer camp our parents envisaged, but they were grappling with more urgent claims: we had reached our teens and it was time to start sifting through the potential partners. My mother will not admit to so banal a motive, but if she secretly hoped to steer me towards some nice Jewish boys, she succeeded all too well.

On my third night in Betar, I was felt up by a nice Jewish boy called Les. I don't know what happened to Les, but it was archetypal experience for me. I was astounded that I was normal enough to provoke this pawing. Years later, I might find myself in bed with one or other bloke who had absolutely nothing to recommend him, except that he had decided that I was desirable. Sheer gratitude was unlikely to inspire a second encounter, but it often explained the first. Of course, I was always aware that relief may be quickly upstaged by regret.

Les got a finger, or was it a thumb? into my Cottontails. Within five minutes I was sure there must be some outward sign of this stain on my character. We were at it again the next night, however, jammed into a foxhole on the perimeter of the campground, grinding away between arguments. Les felt short-changed. With so unexpected a score ('downstairs, inside') on the first night, he imagined that the nights to come would produce significant progress. He was wrong. When he started unzipping himself, I sat up resolutely. The spirit of the times prevailed over the heat of the moment: I saw myself as the reliquary of Les's masculine drives and him as the subject of great, if edited, stories, to tell the girls at school.

Betar's mythology encouraged us to think of ourselves as rebels united in a dangerous cause. The feeling of cama- raderie was as new to me as the sense of intimacy that came from being with people whose origins were more-than-half familiar.

In our first year in Betar, my brother and I spent Sun- days in uniform travelling clear across the city to Allawah, a suburb on the Illawarra line we had never heard of until we received our marching orders from the movement.

To further the cause at Allawah we played ball games with the children, forced them to listen to stories about the heroes of the Irgun, and danced the Hora. Then we made our way to Betar headquarters, in a rundown old mansion at Edgecliff, where eighteen-year-olds subjected us to the same routine.

At atmosphere of anticipation livened up the meetings. Now and again a latecomer burst in excitedly to say that he had been jostled by a couple of creeps who followed him off the bus. The boys who rushed out with him to give chase would come back twenty minutes later, looking crestfallen. It left them conjuring encounters with imagined enemies out of sidelong glances and scraps of conversation. I never heard it suggested that any kid in uniform would have been taunted by other teenagers. It did not occur to us that the natives were more or less unaware of our existence.

Betar gave us a claim on our complicated inheritance. We were Jewish because our parents were, or, to be precise about the counterbalance to assimilation, because Hitler had defined their Jewishness for them: as children of the survivors of the war, we were expected to affirm what our parents had endured by conceding our identity. It was the traditional Jewish equation—if we denied the legacy as they interpreted it, we denied the suffering.

Inevitably engaged in sporadic hostilities with our parents, we meanwhile imagined ourselves to be fighting certain battles on their behalf.

Betar's bloody-minded rhetoric lured some individuals who were anything but joiners, and for them, the organisation functioned much as a street gang—it gave them the excuse to go out looking for likely skirmishes. Eddy Adamek joined Betar when he was twelve. Long afterwards, he was to tell me that if he thought about the war in those days, he could not come to terms with the fact that Jews had acquiesced in going to certain death. What it made him feel about being Jewish, as a child, was a sense of shame, a little lessened by any opportunity for retribution. If someone at Bellevue Hill primary school called him a name like 'fucking Jewboy', Eddy chalked up one for our side.

*

I went to university determined to shake free of the vestiges of my old life and, in the first place, decided to give an impression of great nonchalance. That is to say, I hung the clothes which looked at all respectable in the back of the wardrobe and slouched around from day to day in black stretch pants, a baggy sweater with holes in the elbows and thick, smudged eyeliner. My mother said, 'Your eyes look like pissholes in the snow,' and I accused her of being conventional, the deadliest charge that I could muster. That may have been our final exchange on the matter for several months, because she and dad were going abroad.

Gaudy photos came from Edinburgh and Amsterdam, with postcard blue skies in places famous for drizzle. On the telephone from Denmark, my mother said that all the women in the Tivoli Gardens smoked cigars, and that was the least of her revelations. The cafes all had Royal Copenhagen ashtrays and no-one pinched them, she added, before making an unflattering comparison between the average Australian and the honest Danes. It was a sore point. Very soon after she had opened her dress shop, Paris Frocks, people had stolen the ashtrays in the fitting rooms. She was still sounding nostalgic about life in Europe when her voice faded away. Doubtless dad stood inches away from her, telling her to hang up. The only thing that he ever asked on an international phone call was what time it was, over there. 'Damn,' she shouted at him in Dutch, so loudly that I snapped the telephone away from my ear, '…at uni…'

Perhaps the lines went under water. Gurgling drowned her out. '…ice…ice ends.'

'What?'

'I said…friends?'

'Well, they're not Jewish, if that's what you mean…'

Silence. She would be rummaging around for more coins, but it was too late. We had been abruptly cut off, as usual; the receiver hung from my hand like a dead bird.

'And don't keep asking if they're nice,' I said softly, missing her, 'because they're not.'

*

A Sunday in December 1966: I was at Frensham, a fashionable, if decrepit, private school in a town on the edge of the southern tablelands, about eighty miles from Sydney. The outing provided one revelation after another. Invited to stay for lunch, I found myself at the so-called High Table, on a platform at one end of the dining hall, rubbing elbows with an Anglican clergyman. I was still worrying about the small talk when, with a great scraping of chairs, teachers and schoolgirls alike leaped to their feat. Scrambling up in embarrassment, I kept my eyes fixed on my plate, and remembered having tea with the Turners back in Harbord. The same scoop of mashed potato. The same subservient beans. The same lamb chop, as dried out as the Nullarbor Plain.

'For what we are about to receive,' intoned the pastor, 'may we be truly thankful.' Until that moment, I had been under the impression that grace was said only in nineteenth-century novels. 'Amen.' I had the job. 'Amen.'

During the interview, conducted before lunch in her office, the school principal, Mrs Sandberg, a rangy woman with cropped hair and an ill-fitting intimate manner, leaned forward to confide that she was also from Holland, before asking if I still spoke Dutch.

'Yes,' I said, seeing no need to go into details. It was not a language one might have expected to find useful, in a school on the wrong side of the Great Dividing Range. 'We speak Dutch at home...' The rest of the interview did not take long. I said I could teach English and History. 'How many years of history did you do at the university?' she asked. '...Oh, only one. I'm afraid that's not enough to teach. How many years of English?'

'Two,' I lied, and was immediately hired to teach English to the daughters of the gentry. Though I had been enrolled at the university long enough for the average student to pick up a degree, after the first year I had shifted the focus of my attention to the Piccolo Bar, a Kings Cross hangout for beatniks and drifters, going to so few classes in 1965 that it was only logical to skip the examinations and repeat. But Frensham did not appear to be exaggeratedly fussy about formal qualifications, and Mrs Sandburg also appointed none other than my friend Ina Klein, from Betar, who had dropped out of high school to become an art student.

It struck me as a bit odd that the two of us were to teach in a Christian institution, but we assumed that we had managed to impress the principal, who had gone so far as to make us housemistresses, all for the same forty dollars a week. In thinking it over later, I came to the conclusion that Mrs Sandberg picked me for an easy mark, and she put me in charge of 'West', the school's most ancient pile of perforated brick, where fifty-two girls slept in a dormitory half-sheltered from the elements by canvas blinds.

The school had been founded by a pair of lively, Oxford-educated eccentrics who had progressive ideas about educating the second sex in an invigorating—indeed freezing—environment comparable with an English public school. The vanguard of 1921 had been overtaken (even if the original chill remained), but Frensham's reputation still lured a few blue-bloods whose pedigrees conjured up images of thousands of acres and millions of sheep, images that in turn conjured up actual pupils, from the parvenu families who are the bread and butter of an establishment trading on its association with the ruling class. Indeed, seen from the distance, that is to say, seen from the perspective of parents more preoccupied with the reputation of the school than the discomforts its regime imposed on students, Frensham may have looked just right. Though Frensham is now very different, in those days only a clinician could have expected to meet so many neurotics in the one setting. The dormitory closest to West was run by an overwrought but haunted-looking character, who started conversations by apologising, and then clutched one's arm, as if to cling to something substantial. She was terrified of men, loud noises, the principal and life in general. At night she drank, and was set upon by spectres. In a state of near-hysteria she would telephone, around midnight, to beg one of the housemistresses who lived nearby to chase the prowler supposedly lurking outside her window.

Within the confines of Frensham, this poor, lost crea-ture could just manage to hold herself together, and she was not alone. The school's twittering Old Guard included up to a dozen teachers who could not have survived life on the outside, and whether or not it was the effect of insti-tutionalisation, between them they had so florid an array of tics and twitches that the staffroom at times resembled a sheltered workshop.

The spirit of the school (a kind of Sapphic closet) had infected me after a month or two, and I conceived a pathologically-belated schoolgirl crush on Miss Ferris, the senior mistress, imagining her seated at the edge of my trestle-like bed, wiping my fevered brow. It was a reprise of a fantasy from my childhood, but the former phantoms had been males. Miss Ferris, in contrast, had a pudding basin haircut and a penetrating gaze. She was exceedingly tall, slightly stooped and generally stood with her hands clasped behind her back, like the Duke of Edinburgh on an outing. An intense Roman Catholic, who conveniently taught Latin, she was astringent in style and faintly condescending in manner. I could not bear to call her Beryl.

In first term, when I was still girlishly susceptible, I once shambled over to her in the staffroom. 'Miss Ferris, you have some soot on your forehead,' I said, trying to dab at it, before noticing that she was struggling to express a complicated emotion. It did not seem to be in character for her to declare her feelings toward me, right there, with everyone milling about before Mrs Sandberg crashed into the room, but I had my hopes. Ferris often had an expression of owlish surprise on her long, unlined face, and by now she looked positively astonished.

'It's Ash Wednesday,' she gasped at last. 'Is it?' I said obligingly, wondering what on earth she meant. But I had stopped reaching for her forehead.

*

In the first week of June, Ina and I drove pell-mell from Mittagong, going straight to her parents' flat in Coogee, where we met in secret with our old friends from Betar. Though a number of us had severed all connection with the movement, we were breathlessly caught up in the crisis of the moment. Israel, which had just been mobilised, was on the brink of war and even renegades like myself were more or less prepared to board the next flight to Tel Aviv. Ina, the one exception, was nevertheless involved. She was engaged to a student from Melbourne who was dithering about going, and had turned up to talk it over with her.

No-one else had experienced the slightest doubt. My brother's girlfriend Eve, the English Rose, had already marched in to inform her history tutor at Sydney University that she wouldn't be around much longer because she had to go to war. Of course, there were one or two practical details to sort out first. People had been getting their passports in order, going to Nadel Studios for the passport pictures. Mr Nadel, the Cecil Beaton of Sydney's Jewish community, usually photographed the W.I.Z.O. princesses and the plump little princes whose coming-of-age rated a mention in the *Jewish Times*.

Our sense of urgency was typical. The consensus at the time was that the Arabs were about to make good on their old threat to drive the Jews into the sea. Jews everywhere had been galvanised into action, and at the very time that we met in Coogee, five thousand people crammed into Sydney's Central Synagogue, already jammed to the rafters with cadres of Zionist youth who had marched through Bondi to protest against Arab aggression. The Arabs had not retreated, however, and at the synagogue the feverish appeal for funds was preceded by a gloomy assessment from a politician just back from a junket, who said things looked bad, but the Jews would fight to the end, as they had against the Romans at Masada.

In fact, the first skirmishes of the Six-Day War seemed to be occurring in Sydney, where my brother and his pals from Betar had run up against a bureaucratic juggernaut more difficult to dislodge, as it turned out, than the Egyptian army. In short, Jules and Co were engaged in a war of nerves with the satraps of the State Zionist Council, who claimed the right to act in the best interests of all Jews, and were being more swaggeringly self-important than ever. Outraged to hear that our boys had privately raised the cash to get themselves to Israel as volunteers, council officials had refused to give them the okay they needed to land. 'No sweat,' said Big Ed Adamek, who looked to be in full bloom, even if he insisted on lumbering around the room like a standover man in an Ealing comedy. 'We'll fly to Cyprus and hijack a fishing boat...'

In the end, the fracas with the council went on a day longer than the shindy in the Sinai. The council's war office was in the Maccabean Hall, and having moved into the room next door, the Betarim bivouacked there all week, taking turns to argue with officials and move the coloured pins on the map of Israel they had taped up.

I was to hear about both campaigns at long distance because by dawn, the morning after our meeting, I was navigating the craters of the Hume Highway, stopping only when the radiator boiled over, every half-hour or so, on the way back to Frensham.

That afternoon I went off to the local doctor to have

smallpox and cholera injections. It amused him, for some reason, to be consulted about yellow fever. 'Oh, you're going to the Holy Land...' 'I'm Jewish,' I said, wondering why it always sounded like a non sequitur. 'You still don't have to worry about yellow fever,' he murmured, getting up to show me out, 'and, uh, good luck.'

When the news bulletin came on that evening, I was crouched over the small wireless in my study, feeling faintly ridiculous. The static on the line sounded like gunfire, but then it always did. A BBC voice said, 'The Israeli Ministry of Defence has announced that the Egyptian armed forces launched an attack...' Static drowned him out. '...the Egyptian airforce has repulsed an act of unprovoked aggression by the Israelis, who have lost 432 planes...' Someone knocked on my door. 'Come in,' I screamed. '...three planes...' Kyrsty Macdonald, an engaging, harum-scarum fourth-year girl I liked, stood in the doorway with her friend Rosalyn. 'If you're coming in, shut up for a minute...' I still had my head to the radio, as if listening for signs of life, but the bulletin was over.

'What's happened?'

'How would I know,' I snapped. 'I'm in bloody Mittagong...' It didn't make sense. The Israelis said the Egyptians attacked. The Egyptians said the Israelis attacked. The Egyptians were lying, of course. 'You two want coffee?' Perking up immediately, they chorused, 'Yes, please,' and smiled conspiratorially. On a cold night, I put a little cheap brandy in each cup. How many planes in an airforce? 'The war in Israel's started. This morning, I think.' Stuck in Mittagong with a car likely to conk out for good on the next trip over the Razorback, just as Israel was being wiped off the map.

A couple of days into the war, it emerged that Israel had scored the decisive blow right at the start. The Egyptian airforce pilots had been ready for an attack at dawn, and when it didn't happen, they left their planes and went in for breakfast. 'Listen to this, Ina,' I said, flapping a day-old copy of the *Sydney Morning Herald* at her, and explaining once again that the Israelis had bombed hundreds of the Egyptian planes on the ground, having flown in an arc over the Mediterranean and come in unexpectedly from the north. It was fantastic. Unable to get enough of it, I tracked the Israeli advances on an atlas in the school library. For the one and only time in my life, I identified wholeheartedly with the cause.

*

'So you didn't get there, after all,' said the doctor in Mittagong. It took me a minute to figure it out. The war had been over for weeks, and my fervour had faded into memory. 'No, I didn't. Some of my friends went after the war, and they're stuck in this *kibbutz* out in the desert, getting up at about three in the morning to pick apricots.' The doctor had started doodling on the pad in front of him. 'Of course, that's not what I came about,' I said, deciding to plunge in. 'I'm twenty-one today. Can I have a prescription for the Pill?' He was an urbane, humorous man, but he looked up in amazement, and I may have misinterpreted his expression. 'Just in case.' That time, he laughed out loud.

*

I left Sydney in 1978. I wanted to slow down and take stock, and it wasn't possible in Sydney, where I felt trapped in a role of my own making. I was boyish, boisterous and theatrical. I courted attention and wore costumes, going to parties in a sailor suit, and to work in a second-hand pair of overalls from a Rolls Royce factory in England.

I stopped wearing costumes in New York. I liked being anonymous. No-one cared what I thought, no-one noticed what I did, no-one expected a thing from me. It was as if I were free to reinvent myself. Instead of dreaming up another self, I stubbed my toe against intractable reality and came up against the same old limitations, but I managed to cling to the liberating notion that my life was my own invention.

I saw the city as other than it was, filtering out the public squalor of the present to conjure up a make-believe past, set in the old ghetto on the Lower East Side. The children and grandchildren of the original immigrants had long since fled to the suburbs of Westchester and Long Island, and only a handful of poor, elderly Jews were left. I identified with them, straining at a sense of shared experience I had resisted in Sydney, where acknowledging it risked capitulating to the claims of family and community. In Sydney, I had sealed myself off from my family's past; in New York, I dreamed up connections out of a longing for the past. I left behind my family, imagined myself surrounded by family. Ten thousand miles from home, I felt at home.

After about a year in New York, I went to shul on *Yom*

Kippur, out of curiosity. People strolled into the synagogue in Greenwich Village in blue jeans, and one man was in a pair of shorts, attire which would have created a fuss back in the Temple Emanuel in Woollahra. Instead of pretending to fast (let alone fasting), some of the locals hung around outside, wolfing down slices of pizza before they went in. I didn't stay long, but I made another subliminal gesture towards atonement five years later, going to the Gay Synagogue, where lesbians in prayer shawls played a role usually reserved for men, at least in my experience, by reading out parts of the service. This aside, it wasn't much different from going to shul with heterosexuals or venturing into the Abyssinian Baptist Church in Harlem for a Sunday morning service, because I was an intruder, checking out the customs of the natives. I said that I felt at home in New York. I guess I should have said that you don't have to be Jewish to be a rootless cosmopolitan, but it helps: even now, after eleven years in the New Jerusalem, I need to know that I can pick up and leave, any time at all...

Two Codpieces

Joseph Zaresky

Joseph Zaresky is a lawyer by profession and runs Zaresky Press, a publishing house. Born in 1949 in Sydney, he attended Moriah College and Vaucluse Boys' High. Leaving then for Israel, he obtained a BA at the Hebrew University and was a field medic in the Israeli army. A regular at Sydney poetry readings, Zaresky devised and produced a series of performance programs entitled Oral Stage.

Zvonko

A casual inspection of this sumptuous collection of photographs may well raise the question why it needs an
introduction. Any particular page opened at random will
regale the viewer unfamiliar with Milicevic's work with a
surface not dissimilar to that found in any number of those
magazines, the progeny of *Playboy* and *Penthouse*, that have
multiplied and conquered the earth. In the opinion of this
writer, currently Director of the Museum of Erotic Art in
Osaka, it is in the sheer scale of his enterprise that Milicevic leaps into another dimension. The pages that follow
contain some five thousand photographs whose unique subject is the female genitalia. When one considers that this
was to be the first of one hundred volumes on the same
theme, the mind reels. Yet, ponder this: the unbelievable
goal that Milicevic set himself was nothing less than assem-
bling a documentary of the sex organs of every woman alive.
Even that involved a concession. Do I not recall the evening
we spent together when Milicevic bewailed the accident of
birth that had prevented him from recording the vaginas of
the women of past ages? And the mortality of his own flesh
that was going to rob him of the vaginas of future generations? There was not a hint of whimsy in his manner. I
remember the feeling of being awe-struck in the presence
of an ambition which, in the very act of conquering the

bounds of space, railed against time and human mortality, bounds against which it was powerless.

Zvonko Milicevic died in 1992 in a brothel in Dakar, Senegal. He was struck down by a bullet fired by an armed robber. It appears that the premises were robbed twice weekly by the same person who always took the same percentage of the till (and may therefore be considered a part-owner). Unfortunately Milicevic resisted a demand to hand over his camera, or the film in it, or both. He was aged 43. That roll of film, developed in a police laboratory, has been acquired by the Museum of Erotic Art in Osaka. It comprises 55 exposures. (He used to cut his own film.) From the police documents one gleans that the subjects were employees of the brothel, whether permanent, casual, past or prospective. They were engaged as his models through Milicevic's usual approach.

There were two elements to that approach: fair payment, and respect for privacy. Milicevic was able to draw on a large personal fortune which had been earned by his parents in a business known as Zagreb Studios in a suburb of Sydney. Zvonko's mother had been preoccupied with wedding photography and family portraiture from his early childhood, a fact which he often mentioned, and which may have had a bearing on his artistic obsession.

In addition to payment he always offered to preserve the anonymity of his subjects by devices such as sunglasses, by turning the subject's face from the camera, and especially by selective framing. I believe that Milicevic's need of vast numbers of subjects led to his agreeing with many of them that he would frame part only of the body. Such framing exposed Milicevic to the charge of dehumanisation, often expressed in terms of treating the female body as an object. His response might be summed up as 'a shrug of the shoulders', except that there was no movement of the shoulders, rather a skewing of the large and somewhat doleful eyes and the lax mouth.

To privileged persons (myself included), Milicevic took the trouble to quote, apropos these charges, from the *Ethics* of Spinoza:

> Wonder is the imagination of anything, in which the mind accordingly remains without motion because the imagination of this particular thing has no connection with the rest. (Pt III, *Definitions of the Emotions*, IV)

From the same author (who in diametric opposition to himself had probably never seen a naked woman), Milicevic offered me two further quotes:

> Desire is the very essence of man...(ibid., I)

and

> By the name of desire I understand any endeavours, impulses, appetites, or volitions, which are various, according to the various dispositions of the said man, and often opposed one to the other as a man is drawn in different directions and knows not whither to turn. (ibid.)

I must confess that I am not clear if Milicevic offered these quotes as relating to his own work, or to mine.

For myself, in trying to come to terms with Milicevic's bewildering output, a major problem is that it is virtually unsurveyable. I am using the word in the sense that de Sade is admitted by his most admiring critics to be unreadable. How many photos of this kind can one look at? A very great number, some observers would say. But is there anyone capable of looking at the number that Milicevic actually made, let alone the number that he intended to make? And what, after all, is the point?

I do not pretend to ignore the depressing impression that Milicevic's œuvre may merely be a bizarre illustration to the statement of Octave Mirbeau: '*La femme n'est pas un cerveau, elle est un sexe, rien de plus.*' (Woman is not a brain, she is a sex organ and nothing else.) I prefer to believe that Milicevic was an artist, not a propagandist. What is Milicevic showing us *besides* the endlessly replicated subject matter? The answer is, his own act of replication.

Modern art has a penchant for replication. The *locus classicus* is Warhol. Implicit in such manifestations is a reflection back to photography, specifically to the voracious nature of photography, the technique which we have seen grow into an easily managed though enormous pet devouring reality in the most alarming quantities. Photography prefigured television, which in turn prefigured the personal computer—stages, as is now evident, in the engulfment of human reality by the banal.

I come back to that shrug which was not a shrug. I see it as the gesture of a man who has seen himself threatened with engulfment, and has determined that he was going to do the engulfing. Milicevic refused to be devoured by the mind-numbing monsters of our time. He decided that he too could be a monster, though hurting no one, and therefore became an artist.

The Landlady's Offer

'Mrs Peacock, I may have to leave fairly abruptly. The thing is, I'm wanted by the police. They'll turn up here to arrest me or I'll be gone beforehand. Either way my tenancy cannot last long. This is in lieu of proper notice.'

'You're a wanted man,' she exclaimed matter-of-factly, her head thrown back at a scrutinising angle, then apparently she came to a favourable conclusion: 'Take one of the dogs with you for protection. A gift. They're fighters like no other breed. All those supposedly fierce breeds—the bull terriers, the pit bulls, the Rottweilers, the Doberman pinschers, the German shepherds...*lambs* in comparison with my dogs. "Shark-gripper" is the proper name of the breed. It was bred for hunting sharks. Oh yes, the shark-grippers! What would the industry have been without them? It wouldn't have *existed* without them. *They* were the shark catchers. Every boat had its shark-gripper, one at least, and when a shark was sighted—well before any shark was sighted by the *men*—the dog would hurl itself into the water, swim towards the shark, draw the shark to it, then at close quarters it would bite its teeth into the shark's rump and grip, and grip, and grip! Oh, the stories that were told of those dogs! We bred them—the Peacocks. Those were the days, my friend...when the name "Peacock" was synonymous with shark-grippers. And here I am still breeding them, the poor things! Certainly not for the shark fishery—it's forgotten the shark-grippers as if they'd never existed—but to keep the breed alive. To keep alive the Peacock tradition. There's actually quite a demand for them these days among truck drivers—pick-up truck drivers, tow-truck drivers, all the various truck drivers. It's by word of mouth in their special pubs, their clubs, their CB radio networks, their newsletters, their professional organs. A shark-gripper is noticed on a colleague's truck, inquiry is made, they're referred to me. The phone never stops ringing. I don't have to tell *you*, up there doing whatever work it is you do. Unfortunately there's nothing for it, the truck drivers have to stay in constant touch when they want a shark-gripper. I won't take the pup away from the mother before time, but on the other hand past that time the truck driver will never tame it, the breed's that fierce. Even a day late, it's lost. So they have to ring daily before and after the bitch has whelped. Which is why I'm on the phone constantly. And of course there's always those that know better. They can miss a day or two—the birth will be delayed, or they'll come for it when they're in the area, or they're sick of hearing progress reports of the mother's condition. I have my principles. *If they're late they have to wait for the next litter.* I might offer the disappointed party a whale-gripper instead. It's never accepted, they have their heart so set on a shark-gripper. They'd rather wait for the next litter. Well and good, but there's already a waiting list for the next litter. They have to go to the bottom of the list. Then wait for the howl of protest. They think they should go to the top of the list, not the bottom. They've waited for so long, now this disappointment, it wasn't their fault that they didn't ring or didn't come, there were circumstances beyond their control. There's always some excuse. I've thought about it, and thought about it, and I still think these people should go to the bottom of the list—why should others have to suffer?—but I'm willing to consider any genuine case of hardship. You see there were two breeds that my family bred: one was the shark-gripper, and the other was the whale-gripper. What a breed that was, the whale-gripper! Probably one can never say that any one breed is better than another—all the same, for my money, latching on to a shark is all very well, but latching on to a whale is another matter entirely. Once that dog sank its teeth in a whale, it never let go no matter what. The whale might go berserk, it might dive, leap, somersault, swim at eighty knots for hours, it might do anything it could think of—the whale-gripper stayed with it. And how the whaling men prized them! Did you ever hear of a whaler putting to sea without its full complement of whale-grippers, in the old days? The dogs would go on the boat at the very last, like the special troops, when everything had been checked and double-checked. They'd all be awaiting our arrival, the crew keyed up with expectation, the owners impatient, the captain maintaining cool authority while burning to see what dogs he would get. We'd pull up at the quay and Father would manage the dogs behind the truck, out of view of the crew who were lined up at the rail. That's how they received us, to a man lined up at the rail and at attention. He'd gather the leashes in both hands, the rest of the family helping. Only when he was satisfied with their order and state of discipline, did he allow the dogs to strain forward out of the lee of the truck. Then they appeared, like a chariot drawn by two teams, Father in control and the dogs intent on getting to the boat. And the whole procession moved down the wharf, onlookers crowding in their hundreds and Father in all his glory. I was watching through my tears, I was so proud yet I knew that some of them would never return. Those days are gone forever. We may not like to admit it but they are. The tide of public favour has turned. The whales, the whales, the whales! What about the whale-grippers? That's what *I* want to know. Who's going to save *them*? What international conference has been set up for *them*? Is their blood any less warm? Are they not a mammal? Do they care less for their young? Does a whale-gripper mother not suckle her pups? Does she not teach them how to swim? The poor whales have come to a pass, we know that, I have to say I'm sympathetic too. But does anyone know what plight the whale-grippers are in? You may have noticed my speaking of them in the past tense: "What a breed that *was!*" The truth is, they're all but extinct. All but extinct. They always had a brooding nature, funnily enough—as well as being tenacious they were known for their melancholy. It was as if they were conscious of their destiny. Suddenly nobody wanted a whale-gripper, you couldn't *give* one away. As the numbers dwindled I appealed to institutions here and abroad to accept a breeding pair, but all I got was reasons why they were unsuitable. The real reason was never stated, that they were unfashionable. Politically unfashionable. The politicians and the bureaucrats quietly decided they were an embarrassment. Creatures whose very essence was nobility and self-sacrifice, of course they'd be an embarrassment to these people. The whale-grippers knew they were not wanted, they became fewer and fewer. All there is left of them now is one pair. They're male and female, the right age, but they won't mate. They sense they have no future. I have no right to suggest to them otherwise. If at least a ute owner agreed to take a whale-gripper pup—one of those who'd missed out on their shark-gripper—then I could with justification encourage the pair to mate. But it's always the same with these people. They look askance at the long ears, the drooping dewlaps, the unhappy eyes—the breed is similar to a basset hound in appearance, only with webbed feet—it doesn't fit the image they've got in their mind, regardless of the fact that this is a more tenacious biter than anything they could ever imagine. But try and talk to these people about the exploits of the past. You won't get very far.'

She fixed the tenant with a look which queried whether there was a hope that he might fall into a different category.

'I do recognise the achievements of the past. If it comes to it, I do intend to accept your offer of the ferocious breed, or the tenacious depressed breed, as the case may be.'

The landlady said not a word, but left the room. She returned with two animals; they had no inclination for the visitor, but turned around and wished to leave. The male particularly was resolved, while the female betrayed herself with a backward look. The landlady however harnessed the male with a collar and a leash which she placed in the tenant's hands; and by words and gestures she gave both animals to understand that he had been accepted, all the while working hard to overcome the incredulity which expressed itself in many sidelong glances and shuffling of their peculiarly broad paws. The reluctance born of many rejections finally yielded. The acceptee turned back to the seated tenant and placed a paw on the latter's thigh, which it nearly covered entirely.

'Perfectly adapted,' remarked the landlady.

The tenant reassured her and the animal with a pat. Could there be a better companion in danger than the profound whale-gripper? Of the pair he was inclined to think the bitch would be the better choice. But the landlady would have none of it. Now she led both from the room with a sense of urgency, for what purpose he couldn't imagine, unless it was to give them the satisfaction of revealing their success to the shark-grippers.

That was far from her purpose, as it was far from the traits of the whale-grippers. In due course she reappeared, her face changed, its hard and weathered lines softened, and she herself seeming to be in possession of a great secret. Finally she announced: 'They've mated.' With eyes averted to the floor, she was smiling and nodding: 'O happy day!...Please God the bitch whelps.' In a flurry she brought out two glasses and a bottle of rum. They drank to the dogs' fertility, upon which hung the future of an entire race. For the scion about to set forth with the fugitive, like the whale-grippers of the heroic age, could not be expected to return.

Hansel and Gretel

On the Way to the Operating Theatre

After the Operation

Doris Brett

Doris Brett is a clinical psychologist and writer. Her books include poetry, novels and books on therapeutic story-telling. They have been published in America, Germany, Switzerland, Austria, Russia and Poland as well as in Australia. She has won numerous literary awards: the Anne Elder Award (1984), the Mary Gilmore Award (1985), two John Shaw Neilson Awards (1991, 1994), the Queensland Premier's Literary Award (1994), the Northern Territory Government Award (1995), the Judith Wright Award (1998) and the Gwen Harwood Memorial Award (1998). Her last book of poetry In The Constellation Of The Crab *was shortlisted for the National Book Council 'Banjo' Awards.*

Hansel and Gretel

Each night it begins again
with you in the forest
scattering the crumbs anew.
They lie on the path gathering light
into themselves. If it was dark
they would shine like clues.
They are sharp and dry
like the bones of news
in unattended pages,
hard as small mouths
they long to chatter
on the psychiatrist's couch.

In the candy-bar cage
you lick and lick.
The solicitous witch
comes by. Her eyelids
are limned with chocolate,
her hair has sugar streaks
along the edges.
(Something is wrong with this picture?)

She is in domestic bliss.
She is sweeping up the house
she is cleaning out the oven.
The dinner table's set for two.
(What is wrong with this picture?)

On the cold sugar floor of the witch's house
his face comes back to you
just as he left you
waving and winking
slick as a pill
jolly as a lollipop
(What is wrong with this picture?)
And how did you know he knew?

After that it was easy.
The witch obediently shrivelled
up—dry as a vanilla bean.
The house crumbled like biscuit.
The ghost of the silent partner
though hung around—a smoke stain
in the happy greenery.
And the fire wouldn't stop burning.

Even now it still haunts me,
how if you asked him
he would say
he was only obeying orders,
good as a soldier,
good as an A-OK,
and how now that you know,
although the path winds over and over,
you can never go home again.

On the Way to the Operating Theatre

How strange it is
to see the ceiling go
by like a river.
It smiles at me, sorrowfully
I think. It has been there
for years, silent,
unappreciated—only we
upside-down fliers
on hospital linen
are privileged to see it.

It is white as the moon
and even more secret.
If I study its whorls
and shadows, would it speak
to me? Invite me up
into its vast interior?
I could float up, spreading
the arms of my hospital
gown wider and wider,
and live there,
clean as a fish
and devoid of knowledge.

But the lift swallows us all
up into the whale's
journey, out into a tunnel.
The story pauses.
And now I see:
Here is the room of light.

The red-haired anaesthetist,
the surgeon with gloves
are all waiting.
This is how fairy tales are.
I am the princess in the casket.
They are offering me the apple.

After the Operation

(for Tom)

Some time afterwards
you see the zip
in your body and you begin
to realise what really was done.

You apologise to your body,
you wish it to excuse
such indignity,
after all, it was to save a life.

Your body says nothing.
It trusted you,
believed you would take care
of it, steer it across roads,
avoid fires, not approach
strange men with knives.

'No,' you say. You lift a hand,
your wrist comes into view
pivoting on its ballet-bones
(miracle of miracles)
'It wasn't like that,

I thought of you,' you say,
'before the operation. I pictured
you opening, mysterious flower,
and instead of intrusion,
I thought "hands", "healing hands",
the master gardener tenderly
tending the plants.'

Your body stirs. It's getting
interested. You think of all the slurs,
the sullen chants and incantations
you've poured on it for years—
the workhorse, the slavey, the drear—

and how it's remained faithful,
silently serving your needs,
asking for little: some food and drink,
a simple place in the corner
of your syndicated life.

And how, all the while,
and now you see it,
is the daily miracle,
wilder than flying fish or falling
loaves, the thin exquisite

sheath of bone and blood
the pumping heart and lungs,
the secret liver, the moss
of tissue, the living
muscle's curve. Here

are the networks of nerve—
cathedrals under the skin,
the whole waiting
city beneath the lake
that you wake to deeply
at moonlight while the bells
ring miracle, miracle…

And because there seems
no other word, you say
it again 'miracle, miracle'...
and your body purrs,
hums and begins to heal.

Hopscotch

Brian Castro

Brian Castro is author of six novels include the prize-winning Birds of Passage, Double-Wolf, After China *and* Stepper. *A volume of essays entitled* Looking For Estrellita *will be published by the University of Queensland Press in 1999. Born into a cosmopolitan family which originally settled in Shanghai, he has lived in Australia for thirty-eight years and is currently at work on a fictional autobiography from which 'Hopscotch' is taken.*

Kafka always began with illness. He ached to swim the rivers of Europe but even in the bath, having suffered too much, he could not fake satisfaction; vacillating between doing and writing, between leaping and stasis. His nerves killed him.

Each morning, before dressing, my father practised the Australian Crawl before the mirror. It made him look young, he said, appearing satisfied with his body bent double and flailing in his underpants. He once wrote down thoughts with a gold-nibbed pen and felt too much for this terrible century, assessing the stock market by ticker tape and a thermometer thrust beneath his tongue. At seventy, swollen with memory, he didn't vacillate. He took out his saxophone in a Sydney street and blew a tumour in his brain.

I'm going to tell you this, your father had said just a week before he died. They came from the Kingdom of Galicia and they traded silks in Saragossa, in the old Alcaiceria bazaars. They made the trip each month sustained by learning...that's why I'm telling you this...the importance of that book wrapped in the bolts...you do not need much more than that for the journey.

Your grandfather?

Before him.

Great-grandfather?

Don't be so tiresome, for God's sake.

It was only after some reading that you pinned down this family lore to the fifteenth century. Your father spoke as though that were yesterday. But he had converted and he wasn't going back. You tell him about the red badge of shame they had to wear in 1492; that they could not be addressed as *Don* or *Doña* nor dress in fine clothing. This was respectable anti-Semitism. The worst was yet to come. But your father was not a reader. The only book he admitted reading was Dumas' *The Man In The Iron Mask*. He finished it one day on the ferry between Kowloon and Hong Kong Island and threw it overboard.

Why?

It's been read.

But such a treasure!

All the more reason.

What reason?

There is only one book.

My great-grandfather was Jewish. He was from the county of Lincoln in England and he bore the name of Lee. Or maybe Levi. Or Leve, or Levante. A strapping man with a kindly face and full black beard, he could only sign his name as X. A canny mariner. In Liverpool they mistook him for a gypsy. Then one day he bundled up his family and set sail for Shanghai. Within a few short years he had made a fortune constructing godowns. He set them on piers in the river by importing divers from Japan. Nobody thought of doing that, so ships could sail right up. It was every businessman's dream: a warehouse by the Whangpoo where string bands and two hundred tables lined the jetty with every family birthday. But Great-grandfather's name didn't stand out in China. He assimilated. Paid the gangs and warlords. Didn't make trouble. *You want people to like you*, my father would say many years later, holding up his fist in that way of his which ensured he stood out. People always stared, moved away. Mistook his intentions.

In the 1930s, impoverished intellectuals roamed Shanghai's streets, up to no good. They weren't much as bodyguards or sing-song girls. Penniless professors from Minsk. They read too much and couldn't sell you the dinner off their plate. It's all salesmanship, my father said. A dog at its bowl could make you hungrier. While my father called in his loans they wrote their lives in chalk on sidewalks, bordering them in boxes. You could lay your money on the square that took your fancy; a kind of sport, to play hopscotch over them.

In 1924, in an uncanny inversion of dates, the Spanish government changed a law. Descendants of Jewish exiles from 1492 could once again become citizens. My father converted to Catholicism.

Kafka would have understood the irony. Of something imposed and then released. It made you grateful to discard yourself, like sloughing off a skin. Later, it would do nobody any good. They found dried skins curled in hiding places. It meant you could not speak again...one grain looking like the rest...the rice my grandfather stored. At the first outbreak of hostilites, they broke down his doors.

But even when things were good, my father threw up his fists, a little higher this time, determined that we had to work much harder at respect. Acceptance. He worried I read too much. *Lower your voice*. Play rugger. Pin nudes on the wall, he said. And taking up boxing.

Everyone likes a sport, my mother used to say. But on her side lay Cantonese despair. It would come like rain, pellets of rice or sighs as thick as prayers. Bad rice, bad rice. Never tell a windfall. The next harvest is bound to be bad. *Ah, you know, the rheumatism. That north wind is relentless, your bones can turn.*

Moss grows on one side.

Just as Kafka always began with illness I stay afloat on this repetition with a shining parable on the other side, empty of lesson, save the guarantee that with such lineage, I would never be good at sport.

I think I was born dead. No, not stillborn; the stillness of all creation, and then again, still born forever, missing the interstice. Not that which would make me mendacious; but unbreathing, it would seem, for a long time. I found the world tedious. They extracted half my body weight in phlegm. Now I see it on sidewalks as a cold projection of that familiarity with the universe. By the age of five I had contracted meningitis and was not expected to survive. In a shimmering fever I saw them bringing sweetpeas to my bed, witnessed a hundred candles lit and unlit, was allowed to fondle the golden necklaces of my father's mistresses who lined up in my delirium as saints. *I'll marry you if you can play softball*, they said. The challenge was enticing but the promises never kept, though I ran the dusty pitch at school and crushed the summer into diamonds. Two demons ruled my mind; I could've given in to each, hesitating between life, death and the sweet scent of women.

By eight I was champion of the junior league before the typhus, a mortal finger smoking with conceit, was placed against my temple. Kafka again.

Typhoons and fever. For years my mother took me to our Harvard-educated doctor, a real MD who punctured me with two-inch needles. His assistant shoved medicines through a speakeasy cranny behind which, slatted with light, jars of foetuses stood in ornamental sobriety. Downstairs, a Chinese herbalist swept up crumbs with doleful irony. Always beckoning, he had only snakes to offer, or perhaps discarded umbilicals; we never did enter. Then for months the world was golden, swimming in amber, every book a lighthouse to which I would not sail, my eyes veiled in slow blood-drizzle.

They sent me to Australia where there was sunshine and sport and the smell of cut grass and sea-salt and all those things for which real people yearned. It filled me with an anxiety so dreadful I willed myself an illness. On school runs, I dove to the bottom of rivers and lay glamping at reeds or slipped into sea-caves sounding beneath the thundering tide, released from fury to seek the pneuma of the extraordinary.

When my father left my mother, he lost most of his perfect teeth. He had them pulled to relieve the pressure in his head, no longer did the Crawl, but let out his suits instead.

He liked to fight.

I met him in the street, by an underpass, in characteristic pose. He had no money and was a union picket. Out of his element and fumbling with his lunch in his airline bag, he told me it was lack of faith such things had come to pass. All his friends were wealthy. But they could never have understood the social existence of men. I bought him drinks by the totalizator.

Despite myself I grew stronger; could tolerate more than most my age. My lungs expanded. And then one day, upon completion of twenty laps, a teacher took my pulse. My heart was scarcely beating. He was amazed. I remember the look upon his face, and then the disappointment. Great pulse, he said. (He had expected I would die.) A heartbeat so slow and no Olympic athlete. Then he frowned. Of course, you have to have other things. I didn't have the other things. It was obvious I wasn't quite all there. Never mind, he said, and condemned me to his hypocrisy. You'll live forever. There must be a sport that you can do.

You see, I used to slow my pulse for effect. Holy men and criminals did it just to check on death, to see if they were still in touch or not. It was the sport of crossing over.

I expected them to recur in later life, the demons of the mind and the demons of the body. Things irremediably split. At the begining of each day began the division of body things from mind things. Descartes would have liked to have seen existence cut asunder thus; a deck, some dice; a guillotine. Such neat motions in haphazardness. But the mind has no rhythm of its own. In the wild expanse of involuntary muscle, mystery is habitual. So whenever love crept close it was imperative to run long distances, measuring against each mile the loss of emotion. When good news arrived it was time to sound the oceans, marking off minutes beneath the swell. Success was calibrated in clicking sprockets while cycling every mountain on pure intelligence (the bicycle) and pure muscle (the soul), and drawing closer to the goal of seeking death in health when once a life was found within disease. So without trying, all agony and lesser mortals left behind, it was easy to be competitive; far easier to kill that cowering human thing and soon to realise that whole nations were built on this elimination and in no time, all sensitivity eluded, I was standing in my underpants before the mirror pretending I was boxing.

In 1943 the Austrian writer Hermann Broch was at work eighteen hours a day on something he would never publish.

I've abandoned telling stories because I have a horror of it.

Since Hitler it had become a plague: this rash of stories submerged in inauthenticity and devoid of emancipation. Broch should have done some sport, but that was probably only another form of the same despair he felt when he read all mental illness could be cured by marathon running. It was an idea you could sell.

They forgot to add you had to run forever.

Day after day after gumtree sporting day I drew lines across pages and made them into boxes oblong and rectangular until I heard the first celestial creaking; the door to blue extinction. I took a drag at a cigarette then, and left the country.

On a stretch of estuary where I was once brought to life, jetfoils, helicopters and insects skim. Headlands rise from dirty mist at twilight, while a ragged nightlife jumps in counterpoint against the pulse of motor launches, neon and cocaine. A fetid breeze fans different competition now; it is not gratuitous. My heart pounds. Absorbing a damp illness, I begin to recognise these sharper rhythms as my own. And so with writing.

Next afternoon my cousin takes me to visit graves. It is Ching Ming, time for grave-sweeping. My cousin is Eurasian and very beautiful and she keeps to these traditions of her father's. The hillside slopes precipitously towards water. I watch her light incense, sense her hips against the rounded stone and feel an equal tension of desire and respect, and then I watch the sea and see in its changing colours her soft, soft lips. On the next afternoon I return alone. Each afternoon after that. As always, I see five or six women working below in the shade of beach umbrellas. They are sorting bones. Cleaning, selecting for size, breaking longer pieces up. They burn the wood, char the skulls, hammer them in. I realise only later the umbrellas were not for comfort, but to conceal the disinterment. On another hillside I find neglected markers of long-dead relatives. My uncle Jaime Guimereis, Far East boxing champion who once had a medicine ball filled with shot and punched it back and forth. My great-uncle Antonio Ribeiro, the swimmer of islands, who, at the turn of the century, breast-stroked his way through shark-infested waters to fulfil an obsession of gigantic proportions. He, too, had lost his love. My own grandfather Bonifacio, long-jumper extraordinaire, who leapt from one ship to another and fell between. And on the other side, balletic, opium-infused Uncle George 'Woodpecker' Wing, whose mathematically placed, gracefully batted shuttlecocks once earned him the doubtful sobriquet of *The Butterfly of Badminton*.

in the 1960s
an artist by the name of edward kienholz
created what he called concept tableaux
he sold you a concept for a third
of the actual building cost
of what you could have had made
a sculpture or an installation
and since you owned the concept
described on an 8½ × 11 inch piece of paper
its title engraved on a brass plaque
you could do the same with lives
marked out on a footpath
when theyre worth much less
not even a third of a concept
i wrote to kienholz i said ed
give me a sample of the sporting life
since i cant afford
the concept of redemption
he sent me back an 8½ × 11 inch piece of paper
on which was drawn
a line
a scratch
a scotch
its where you cross
you understand
that counts he said
the crisis of conscience or the greasy palm
the vacillation or the vaseline
and hey
some of us never grow rich

I made a brass plaque and screwed it onto my father's grave, long untended. They had all but forgotten who he was. The night before he died he had a party. I regret nothing, he said, and took my girlfriend to the pub. I sat down on the stone and drew my linked squares. That night he told her something he never told me. That he liked my writing. For what it's worth, I mean, he said. A chill wind was at my back and in my dream of illness I heard the roaring. They once laid their bets on him before all was scratched. A bit each way. I was the only one who took it to the line since the all or nothing was his own advice. In 1929 my father was the top jockey in Shanghai.

I stand atop his grave and gaze at his residual repertoire and learn from here what Kafka knew instinctively: that all uniqueness stems from the prohibition of victory; that there was now only the hollow matter of

the hop,

step

and jump.

The *Bar Mitzvah* of a Nazi

Alan Jacobs

Alan Jacobs was born in Sydney in 1948. He lectured in creative writing at TAFE colleges, and conducted many writing workshops, editing a literary magazine of his students' work as well as featuring them on a community radio programme. Alan has written numerous short stories and articles and has been published in Quadrant, Subterranean, Generation Magazine, *and the* Australian Jewish News, *among others, as well as in overseas publications. He is also an inveterate organiser of poetry and short story readings in cafes, bookshops and libraries. His other life includes filmmaking, developing museum exhibitions and travelling.*

THERE ARE SOME JEWS, you know, who were Nazis.

A small group of 'Jewish Nazis' existed in Germany during the thirties. The Naumann Group. Their official name was the Association of Nationally Minded German Jews. They supported Hitler, actively, and their slogan was '*Raus Mit Unz*', 'Out With Us'. They sought a place for themselves in the Third Reich. Though their organisation was outlawed, many of them refused to leave Germany. In 1943 they were deported to the east, where they were gassed.

I am the son of a Jewish Nazi. My father was more of a closet Nazi—he saw no clash between his religious and political beliefs, except in public.

I don't know if my father had been a member of the Naumann Group. He never told me much about his former life in Germany. I do know that like many German Jews, my father, who'd attended high school during the Weimar Republic, was imbued with German nationalism by right wing teachers incensed by the Allies' treatment of their Fatherland. If my father had been a member of the Naumann Group he certainly kept that a secret. Anyway, he didn't stay in Germany; he came to Australia in 1937. A reffo. His parents died in the Holocaust—in Theresienstadt. Yet during my childhood there was an abundance of evidence that definitely exposed his clandestine obsession with Nazism.

For one thing Hitler was always present at the dinner table. Especially on Sundays when he'd share the pea soup and *bratwurst*. He was my father's companion, his pal. Like James Stewart's invisible rabbit in the film *Harvey*. My mother was never at ease with his presence.

Another thing: my father sang flagrantly nationalistic German songs—'*Deutschland Über Alles*' a definite favourite—whenever he took a shower. Sometimes a rousing marching song would come bellowing from the bathroom to invade the entire house. That voice would reverberate around the walls, causing them to tremble and shake. And tremble and shake was what I did, for wherever I sought refuge it was to no avail. Those stirring numbers clobbered me into a state of awe and frightened me into submitting to his every command: TURN ON THE SHOWER! GET ME MY TOWEL! MORE SOAP! (He believed that the soap was made from Jewish remnants and took great pleasure in richly lathering himself.) Fortunately he was European, so those showers were only a weekly event. I began to wonder, at an early age, how Dr Mengele and Martin Bormann kept up such European habits, living as they did in tropical climes.

Details of top-ranking Nazis were drilled into my skull as soon as I could listen. I knew, as soon as I could utter 'Pa Pa', how to pronounce the words 'Adolf Hitler'. During the following months my education consisted of learning to pronounce other difficult words too—each with the exact German diction: 'Goebbels'; 'Goering'; and 'Himmler'. The latter name was not so difficult to master, sounding as it did like 'Hitler', though at first I did have trouble with the 'Heinrich' bit.

As soon as I could move about on my legs, he had me goose-stepping all over the living room carpet; my little limbs stretched outward to their limits as this peculiar form of discipline was handed out from father to adoring son. Mother was horrified at the spectacle of her little boy following his father around, aping such ghastly movements. But a sharp '*HALT DEN MUND!*' or, if that didn't work, a swift backhander stifled any protest or outburst she might have gasped.

Each time my father entered the kitchen for breakfast he greeted me with a curt '*SIEG HEIL!*', accompanied by a neatly executed slapping together of the heels of his slippers. After a short time I came to appreciate that to win my father's favour I would have to emulate that salutation. So when he arrived home at night or whenever he entered my bedroom—which was often, to provide me with as much practice as possible—I would immediately leap up, click my heels and thrust my arm toward the ceiling, snapping '*SIEG HEIL!*' and enunciating it perfectly.

These rites, I was instructed, were never to be divulged to anyone outside our house: the threatened punishment being a prolonged stay inside our large gas oven. After all, my father was an important man in the community, and in the public eye we were practising Jews.

Most doctors when they come home at night tend to rest and relax after a hard day's work. Not my father! The light would burn on in my bedroom for hours while he perused books from his library of works by and about Nazis. He kept his books in my room to conceal his surreptitious fascism from visitors to our house. Like a zealous professor of history he would study *Judgement at Nuremburg*, shaking his head in disbelief, pore over the passages of *Mein Kampf*, muttering, 'Brilliant, brilliant, the man is a genius!' or he would feast his gluttonous eyes upon his bibles of Hitlerian biography: Bullock and Shirer.

Many hours, dedicated hours, he would devote relating stories to me about the actions and achievements of the Nazi greats. While other children blessedly received bed-time stories about Donald Duck or the Cow that Jumped Over the Moon, I was being instructed in the philosophy of Nietzsche, forced to listen to recorded speeches of Hitler and Goebbels (my father dreamily nostalgic) and I was inoculated with intimate details of the rituals of the SS. Even as I commenced primary school I knew how the Nazi Party was formed, the life story of the *Führer*, as well as the general history of the Third Reich.

'A perfect gentleman in the surgery,' was the way many people described my father at work. I witnessed this myself whenever I was there: adoring patients, devoted nurses, fellow practitioners dispensing their praise. Yet my mind was vivid with fantasies of what must have occurred behind the closed doors. He never said much about it, but my father often referred to his consultations with his largely Jewish clientele as 'experiments'. Often he would write long letters to various South American destinations, and receive even longer replies. Communications of this kind were passed off as correspondence with professional colleagues.

The crisis of conscience came when I was thirteen— the year one becomes a man according to Jewish tradition. A festering hatred of all things Jewish had been fed to me the previous year during which my father introduced me to the Nazi theory of Political Biology. Insisting that this was imperative for my education, he nevertheless calmly proceeded to prepare me for Jewish manhood. Weekdays I was heavily indoctrinated in Nazi tenets; Sundays I was driven to the synagogue for *Bar Mitzvah* lessons. He took great care to adhere to all other outward signs of embracing his religion: he never worked on Saturday; *Rosh Hashonah* and *Yom Kippur* always found my father deep in public prayer at the synagogue; and he always contributed generously to the Blue Box collections for Israel.

All this I accepted. To be Jewish and simultaneously to steep myself in a knowledge of Nazism, as well as its trappings: songs, salutes, steps of geese. Though I did not realise it yet, somehow my tender twelve-year-old brain could not reconcile the ambivalence of *Bar Mitzvah* lessons and Nazi racial theories. I hated my teacher of the *Torah*. I began to look down on Jews in our neighbourhood, and to boycott all known Jewish shops. At night I would climb out of my window and hurl stones through the bedroom windows of Jewish households. Why? In order to scare them out of copulating: in this way I hoped to single-handedly prevent the growth of Jewish numbers in our area. And at times I pilfered the milk money of Jewish families—especially when Father's Day or the *Führer's* birthday approached—so I could buy my father more mementoes of Nazism.

Over the years my mother had become afraid of me and lived in mortal fear of her husband. We would take turns at beating her black and blue, sometimes using a magazine, sometimes a school ruler. Nothing really lethal because my father was a respected man in the community, a gentleman—and I was his son. I'm not sure my mother actually enjoyed the beatings; she never complained about them. After all, she basked in her status as the doctor's wife, and would never think to leave him.

*

The day of my *Bar Mitzvah*. Expectant family friends and influential Jewish patients—all ignorant of my father's political beliefs—filled the synagogue seats that Saturday morning. The rabbi, despite my contempt for him, had been extremely impressed with my progress as his student and eagerly looked forward to my perfect reading from the *Torah*. Not one soul in that house of prayer knew of my secret disdain for Jews. Not one soul, that is, apart from my father, who still held over me the threat of that lethal dose of gas should I reveal anything in public.

Proud, glowing faces amid glittering diamonds watched me as I began to read my passage from the holy scriptures. It was like music to their Jewish ears. One listener in the front row nodded appreciatively like a devotee of a symphony orchestra. Ladies swelled with pride and satisfaction, reflecting on the *naches*, the special joy, I was giving my deserving parents.

After my reading on the Pharaohs and the Exodus, I abruptly stopped and surveyed the congregation. Hook noses floating in a sea of crinkly hair. Sitting to my left, my father beamed his approval, his glee.

'Pharaoh should have exterminated the Jews!' I screamed at the top of my lungs.

I couldn't help myself, could no longer contain the conflict within.

'Another Hitler will come!' I yelled maniacally, articulating the fear of each and every astonished person in front of me. 'Another Hitler will come and all of you who missed out the last time will be as lambs to the slaughter!'

My words were promptly punctuated by a resounding click of the heels and a voice-straining '*SIEG HEIL!*'

The rabbi rose from his seat, turned several shades of purple, and began to convulse, shaking uncontrollably like a wind-up toy. He shrieked, clutched at his chest and dropped to the floor, face contorted in agony. The victim of a massive heart attack.

MY FIRST JEWISH VICTIM!

Awe-struck, I looked to my father for approbation. He was slumped in a state of shock. Frothing from the mouth, he was helplessly struggling to control his arm from shooting skywards. The audience was scattering everywhere, right and left, over the benches of the seats. Pandemonium had broken out as they surged toward the doors. Within a minute I was standing alone in the synagogue—except for my father, by now in a cataleptic state, the deceased rabbi, and several Jewish bodies, trampled to death in the frantic rush for the exits.

Fearing punishment from my now twitching father I bolted out of the synagogue; right through the terrified crowd I ran, out onto the streets, and away to the sanctuary of the local Nazi Party. Arthur Smith, in those days the Australian *Führer*, had no idea what to do with a thirteen-year-old Jewish Nazi and handed me over to Dr Barnardo's Home for Children, where I spent an unhappy adolescence.

After many years I learned of the fate of my poor mother. She'd been mortified in front of her friends, not to mention the important Jewish patients, and she'd committed suicide immediately afterwards. She threw herself into the large gas oven in her kitchen. My father was admitted to an insane asylum and was only recently released. I have never dared see him, even to this day. I understand that he opened up a small restaurant somewhere in this city, serving German cuisine. *Bratwurst* and pea soup. An Australian version of Aschinger's in Berlin, a favourite haunt of his student days. It is in an old railway carriage, and just like Aschinger's there are no tables. Standing room only. The Cattle Car Restaurant. It is patronised by the surviving German Jews of his generation. I believe business was good, though now it is literally dying off.

Though I still have a desire to see my father again, I don't know if it is only to taste the pea soup and German sausages of my childhood.

The *Bar Mitzvah* is a joyous occasion, an important rite of passage, a ceremony which should remain in the memory forever. Mine was no exception. Even though I sacrificed my *Bar Mitzvah* presents (briefcases, pen and pencil sets), I feel satisfied that I remain true to my convictions, to the priceless education my father had bestowed upon me.

The Wailing Wall

Hot Date

Dorothy Porter

Dorothy Porter has published ten books, including three verse novels, five collections of poetry and two novels for young adults. Her most recent book is the verse novel What a Piece of Work. *Her best known book is the crime thriller in verse* The Monkey's Mask, *which is currently being adapted for film. She is currently working on a new collection of poetry.*

The Wailing Wall

The skin on my hand
    last night
glowed olive-dark
    from the cuff
        of a white silk shirt

distracting me

I watched it
    with a slow narcissism

I watched it
    holding a drink
I watched it
    still and mysterious
        on my heavy leg

and once again
    I couldn't talk
        to my dead grandmother

even to say
    thank you
for my gypsy hand

that is bloody useless
but good to look at
under a soft lamp

good
    for waving prettily
        in the air

thank you, Gran
I'm sober now

thank you
    for giving me
        your skin

my skin

you were darker
    darker
        than me

what did you call it
    in others?

this darkness
this skin that glows
    under a light

black blood, black blood

who were you
    prickling in your skin?

what did you do
    with your small dark hands
        that could sew, cook, crochet
            and prune a rose

that never talked
　　like some jabbering foreigner
　　　　in the air

that bunched in gloves
　　drove a car,
　　　　when women didn't drive,
that bunched in fists
　　sat like stones
　　　　on your lap

they were useful hands, Gran

they worked for you
　　like sullen slaves

on their own time
　　they had other business

old, old business

they were stiff-necked hands
it didn't matter
　　that you denied them
　　　　their temple, their people
　　　　　　their strange
　　　　　　　　and domineering place in the world

they knew their birthright
they knew what to do to you

didn't you ever notice
　　the veils over your mirrors?

didn't you ever notice
    the discreet tear
        in your perfect clothes?

they were at work
        your hands, your hands
            were sitting *shiva* over you

Hyman, Cohen, Aarons, Meyer
    and Brodziak

Nathan, Saartje, Aloe, de Leeuw
    and Leefson

your fingers had circumcised names
    your hands muttered them
        like curses

so what did you curse
    while they cursed you?

you cursed your skin
your dark skin   your dark skin

you cursed it
    wherever you saw it

you cursed it
    in Africa

you cursed it
    in a migrant face

you cursed it
    in your grand-daughter

with her useless hands
   that glowed at night
     like your hands

    your busy hands.

Hot Date

Pine trees
    come most alive
        dripping with resin
            in a fire

I've got a hot date
    with Death

will she be
    my boiling Celt?

will we dare
    the White Horses?

dewy together
    Death and I

hot-sea blue

or will Death
    be my curly corkscrew
        Jew?

'I'm you
I'm you'
she moans

knocking me to the floor
of an old blood hotel
sucking out my breath

Oh Death!

I never knew you
 in a dress
 in high heels

just the melt
 of your breasts
the forklift
 of your tongue

I can't bring home
 a devil
   to meet my mother

but I won't
 ring for a taxi

I'm not leaving

until you tell me
 about yourself

 let's talk, Death

can't we be friends?

is it all
  sex
   with you?

do you like cricket?
do you like tennis?

what did you think
 of this year's Film Festival?

Sip your long black
    slowly, Death

I want to know you

do you want
    to be my second cousin
        twice-removed?

Celt or Jew.

You'll never be English, Death

I said Goodbye To All That
    with my last Anglican
        Communion

I can't remember
    the wafer
I couldn't get drunk
    on the wine

Celt or Jew.

Breath or dew.

You'll never be faithful.
I'll never be true.

Because, Death,
    I'm not simple

and neither are you.

History in the Kitchen

Rosa Safransky

Rosa Safransky's writing has won an Age *Short Story Prize, the ABC Bicentennial Short Story Prize and* Canberra Times *National Short Story Award. Her work has been anthologised in Australia and overseas by Transworld, Oxford University Press, Allen & Unwin, UQP, MUP, Deutsche Taschenbuch Verlag, Simon & Schuster, Harper Collins, University of Nebraska Press, Spinifex and Australian Short Stories. Safransky's novel,* Bonjour Brunswick!, *was nominated for the Harper Collins National Book Council Award and she was awarded a Fellowship by the Literature Board of the Australia Council. She is currently working on a novel called* The Fax of Life.

MY FATHER LIKED TO pluck world leaders out of thin air and sit them at the kitchen table. Or stand them in front of the huge wooden ironing board my uncle Emil built, shortly after we arrived from Paris. I was almost certain the ironing board was alive, as I watched my father vigorously pummel coats and dresses across its sturdy shoulders. His expert fingers sent glittering evening gowns flying across broken floorboards as he pondered world events, each time he returned from the toilet at the end of the backyard, his newspaper clenched tightly in his fist. He is Hitler, Khrushchev, the Pope, Eisenhower, Menzies and Churchill. He is the Suez Canal, Parliament, Congress and the Kremlin. He is the KGB and the CIA. He is behind the Iron Curtain, he is jumping over the Berlin Wall as he pulverises every stray crease from a mountain of coats heaped on the floor. The heavily frayed electrical cord writhes to and fro as his iron lunges at a sleeve, drowning the tiny workroom in the stench of scorched taffeta. An assortment of garments spring to life each time he charges at them beneath the bare light bulb suspended above the table.

'What do Australians know about the Holocaust?' My father smashes the kitchen table with his fist, yelling at the herring, yelling at God, while my mother stands silently at the sink. He looks like a gaunt version of Nikita Khrushchev at the UN, pounding the rostrum repeatedly with his shoe.

'I don't want YOU to forget!' He shakes a finger at me, even though I wasn't around during the war. Besides, my ear is pressed so tight to the mantel radio that sits on the floor it would take an oxyacetylene torch to pry us apart. My father is no longer in our kitchen. He is in 'AUSHVITZ'. An SS officer points 'right', 'left', 'right', 'left', with a stick. He pauses.

'What is your occupation?'

'Auto-mechanic.' My father's words fly out of his mouth, he doesn't know how, as he returns to our kitchen for a moment to confide to my mother and me, 'In 1944, they didn't need tailors any more.'

'Right!'

My father is herded into a shower. These showers kill lice, the same lice my mother finds in my hair and crushes with her fingernails during a lice epidemic at school. Why can't he stop shouting? His eyeballs are popping out of his head as he chokes on a piece of herring lodged deep in his throat. I want him stripped of all his 'father medals' and deported as far away from our kitchen as possible. I need a magic spell to capture him in a matchbox, like a grasshopper or a praying mantis, and spirit him into my mother's kitchen cupboard with the sagging wire mesh. To bolt the tiny wooden door with the crooked latch and command the endless roll of cotton wool, the container of boric acid, the thermometer in its shiny metal case and the stockpiles of Redhead matches to keep him under strict surveillance.

I hate the battalions of red, orange, green and purple pills that invade every meal. My father's body is a War Zone and my mother its Chief of Staff. She mixes medications, prepares special diets, concocts ointments in saucepans on the stove. Her kitchen is a laboratory. Instead of noodles, she boils radium. The stove glows in the dark. My father swallows the lot and knocks back a brandy. My father is the guinea pig, my mother the Mad Scientist. She takes copies of *The Lancet* that belong to the retired optician next door. She takes them from the garbage and reads them in bed. She tests her latest theories, her wildest ideas.

'I need a new body,' my father groans.

'Give me something to do,' I plead in my invisible voice as I kick the laundry sink repeatedly with my shoe. My mother's knuckles are white and beads of sweat coat her forehead as she engages in hand-to-hand combat with my father's shirts, scrubbing them relentlessly in the cement sink in the back shed. She punches the bed sheets and pillowcases as if she were wrestling with a giant squid, letting its tentacles spread out before her, then plunging her arms straight through its heart. The creature almost drags her to the ocean floor, but she twists its neck into a huge plait and heaves its lifeless body into a plastic bucket standing on the ground. I wish I was a giant squid. I wish I was a giant 'anything' as my father chases me round the clothesline.

'Why did you run away?' His belt bites into my legs.

'I didn't run away. I was playing in the park!' I dodge under a towel.

'I'll teach you not to answer back!' The bright blue vein on his forehead throbs dangerously. 'I've got to change your CHARACTER before it's TOO LATE!' He charges. I duck. He misses. My mother watches. Pleads with him. I race into the shed and bolt the door. Hard! He yells. Curses. Storms into the house. The flywire door on the back verandah slams shut. I didn't run away, no matter how many times my parents insist I did.

I watch and listen through cracks in the shed. Gnarled trunk of nectarine tree. Slivers of bras and underpants. No one there. Unbolt the squeaky lock, tiptoe past the clothesline, daisy bush, plum tree, squeeze through the back fence and escape down the back lane. Hide in houses condemned by the Board of Works. Old laundry. Cement troughs. Cobwebs. Spiders. The cat finds me. The cat knows where I am. The little traitor leads the way, closely followed by my mother.

'Come home and say sorry to your father. You know he loves you and he believes in God.' No he doesn't. He's too pissed off at God. But it's dark. Cold. I follow them home. Spill out words I don't mean. Plant an empty kiss, at my mother's insistence, on his cheek. My real words get stuck in my throat.

No matter what I do, I'm always in trouble. Even as my mother grabs my hand, clutching the basket of food in another and we run down the ramp to the train waiting in the dark, my legs have trouble keeping up. The saucepan of hot barley soup rattles noisily against a jar of apple compote, buffeted by a loaf of rye bread peeking through the dishcloth my mother uses to keep my father's dinner hot. There is even something eerie about the sepia photos of the bush swaying above our heads as the train plummets past graffiti shrieking, 'STOP THE BOMB!' and 'MENZIES OUT!'

When I smell the liquorice factory, I know we're there. My mother thrusts my hand deep in her pocket as she flies through the empty station. But I always slow her down. I force her to stop in front of the bright lights on the marquee of the Hoyts Regent, hypnotised by a billboard of *The Rains of Ranchipur*. Tiny people topple head over heels into a crack in the earth while an enormous Indian prince in a white turban embraces a giant blonde woman. '**LanaTurnerEarthquakesMonsoonsCinemascope-Technicolour**' fade into a blur as my mother sprints past the theatre rattling her saucepans like kettledrums. She moves so fast, even Superman couldn't keep up with her.

'Is it a bird? Is it a plane? No. It's **S-U-P-E-R-M-A-N!**' I chant along with the radio as I propel myself across the factory floor, hanging onto a chrome dress rack, till I collide with a tailor's dummy standing to attention in the middle of the room. An ensemble my mother spent hours meticulously beading explodes, spraying the floor with iridescent sequins. My father makes a fist at me and I beat a quick retreat up the old staircase. Except for a bare light bulb, the storeroom is almost dark. Empty cigarette packets, twisted bundles of zippers, boxes of sewing threads, buttons and packets of tailor's chalk are scattered across cutting tables. Coat-hangers secured with strips of fabric are piled high on the floor. Thick layers of dust cover the brown stains on the peeling wallpaper, the cracks in the ceiling, even the spiders industriously spinning their webs. Dust is the Secret Police of the room. Dust covers the bolts of cloth stamped 'Tokyo' and 'Taiwan' in bright gold lettering, stacked in pyramids across the floor, where I spend hours scrutinising old fashion magazines that show what college girls wear to socials when they go out with clean cut boys called 'dates'.

My eyes are shut. I am Joan Collins in Technicolor. The star of *The Girl On A Red Velvet Swing*, a film I saw at the Hoyt's Regent, where a real swing is strung above the marble staircase with scores of autumn leaves scattered round the foyer. The plaster chickens suspended on steel hooks in the poultry shop across the road are invisible. So are the men in white hats and blood-spattered aprons unloading squawking chickens from a van as I soar across the theatre, scattering flowers to my admirers the way Joan Collins does in the movie.

'Are you for sale?' A dark shape knocks loudly on the factory window. My swing evaporates in mid-air as the front door opens and footsteps disappear into the back room, where my father is listening to a political commentator he loves abusing while he irons.

'Is she for sale?' the voice asks again, as I stand frozen next to the dusty Christmas tree that hangs in the window all year.

'Who?' My father sounds surprised.

'Your daughter.'

'I would never sell her,' he laughs.

I have no idea of the number of hours I spend in the factory at night, as I run late to my punctuality obsessed, electric bell ringing school next morning. At school, I'm always 'in trouble' for 'talking'.

'SILENCE!' Evil Eyes yells. 'I want to be able to hear a PIN DROP!' He grabs my arm and throws me out of the room. I am the fifth grade stand-up comic. I spend hours perched on a chair doing 'Evil Eyes' pin-dropping impressions in the kitchen mirror. Giggling is the only thing that punctures my family's driven industriousness. Uncontrollable fits of giggling, till tears run down my cheeks.

'She'll wet herself.' My mother's voice acquires its metallic edge and I laugh even harder. My father looks uneasy. A warning note in his voice alerts my mother: it's time I went to bed.

I can't sleep. I lie awake on the couch in the living room, frightened of the shadows the moon casts on the wall. Even the carved black elephants on the mantlepiece look threatening. So does the darkness in Uncle Leon's room, when he is not there to flick on the brass switch with its friendly 'click'. The only light comes from moonlight seeping through our agitated lace curtains. I finally gather up my quilt and tiptoe to the door of my parents' room. They are alive. I can hear them breathing. I steal into their room, spread my quilt on the floor and lie down at their feet. Moonlight, shattered by my father's snores, slides off the silver weatherboards next door, making the cupboard and the bed with the wire spring dip in the middle, rock to and fro. Or is it my father's snores propelling the creaking furniture around the room I panic, as I trace the zigzag pattern on the cold linoleum with my fingernail?

The wind slams our rusty wire gate with its squeaky hinge, open and shut. The heavy branches of the tree in our front yard always threaten to crash through our ceiling. Our house looks lopsided like it's had a stroke. The front windowpane is cracked; someone tossed a brick through it. A huge lion guards our fireplace. My mother's personal lion. It leaped into her hands when our ship, on its way to Australia, reached the Suez Canal. Its face is deeply furrowed and its eyes are fixed on some invisible prey lurking on top of the china cabinet. I know there was a lion. I'm sure of it but a snapshot of my Uncle Leon reading a copy of *Pix* shows a camel. Did our lion leap over the china cabinet and escape back to Africa? Or was it prowling somewhere round our tiny living room, which for some reason we called the 'big room'? Would it be joined one day by Leon's herd of carved black elephants which roamed the mantlepiece? How did Leon get from Poland to Italy before he materialised in the bedroom next to the living room where I sleep?

My family dates time from the moment my father and uncle re-united in Melbourne. The last time they saw each other was in Auschwitz. It got into *The Sun*. People talked about it on trams. Conductors, drivers, passengers, ticket inspectors. All the trams were talking. All over Melbourne. Moreland Road. Sydney Road. St Kilda Road. Everyone knew about us. I wave to surprised strangers at tram stops till my mother tells me to stop. My family burst out of a clamshell like Boticelli's Venus in one of the art books Leon kept in a suitcase under his bed.

My Uncle Leon **NEVER** talks about the past. Never mentions Poland. The only Polish thing about Leon is he speaks Polish but not to us, we live in a Polish Speaking Free Zone. Although my parents speak fluent Polish, they only use it when they don't want me to understand what they are saying. After I exhaust my vocabulary of *leszak*, *lalka*, *dzenkuya* and *dovidzenya* ('deck chair', 'doll', 'thank you' and 'goodbye'), I am linguistically at sea. Normally we stuck to our secret language, 'Yiddish'. We spoke in invisible ink.

And why does my father keep a book in a yellow dust jacket called *The Scourge of the Swastika* in the glovebox of the car? A group of emaciated figures crouch in the shadow of a pair of giant jackboots on the front cover. A tractor bulldozes naked corpses, piled on top of one another, into huge ditches. Women run stark naked, watched by uniformed German officers. An oven door is left wide open, revealing the charred remains of a human skull inside, and an ugly woman called Ilse Koch is pictured above a photo of two charred, shrunken heads.

'**I was in a cattle truck!**' my father yells in the kitchen. 'When they opened it, corpses fell out. The sky was red. We couldn't see the stars. 'Au-shvitz' was full of the smell of human flesh burning.'

'Don't listen,' Leon whispers. 'It's only your father.'

How can I not listen? The kitchen is the size of a matchbox. When my father smashes the table with his fist, the lace doileys impaled under the glass jump. My mother's green glass dish somersaults off the table, while the herring makes a straight trajectory for the ceiling. The soup bowls turn into unmanned space shuttles, as the *lockshen* rendezvous with the rye bread, which has gone into orbit around the kitchen. Our kitchen is surrounded by barbed wire, dogs, machine guns and whips.

'HURRY! HURRY! HURRY! If you didn't go quick they shot you in the back.' My father's head is completely shaven. He wears a striped baggy suit and a striped hat. He is yelling so loud, I've stuffed my fingers in my ears. The more he shouts, the more deafening my mother's silence becomes. He smashes his fist against the wall and the light bulb goes out. My father vanishes. He's in a bakery in

Czechoslovakia. A salami hangs around his neck and he's stuffed three loaves of bread down his throat. He is swollen from hunger. He occupies the entire kitchen. It's 1945. White flags wave from every building. Hitler's been dead for a week. But Hitler isn't dead. The war hasn't stopped. Our kitchen is a Round Up, a Selection, a Death March. '**K-R-R-U-P-P-P-S**!' Munitions Factory in Germany.

'**How could a god let six million Jews perish in the gas ovens?**' my father thunders. His voice is cryogenically frozen. Our kitchen is etched in my brain with nitric acid. I huddle over the mantel radio, my feet bolted to the floor. The cat brushing itself against my mother's legs has turned to stone. My father is a waxwork in Madame Tussaud's. My mother lights a candle and the wax starts to melt.

Somewhere there is a photo of my father in a drawer, with a compass needle I plunged through his heart. I am not a Haitian Voodoo Queen and he is not a Zombie. Still, he must have felt a twinge. A tiny earth tremor. A seismic hiccup. He felt nothing. He was too busy fighting history in the kitchen.

Flying in Silence

Judy Horacek

Judy Horacek is a freelance cartoonist and writer. Her cartoons appear fortnightly in The Australian Magazine. *She is the author of three cartoon collections,* Life on the Edge, Unrequited Love Nos. 1–100, Woman With Altitude *and a book of cartoons and writing called* Lost in Space. *Her next cartoon collection,* If the Fruit Fits, *is being published by Hodder Headline in October 1999.*

THE PAST IS MADE up of pictures, like stills from movies or scenes from period dramas. You wonder at the sepia world where all the men are chiselled and all the women are fragile.

At the wake after my grandfather's funeral, my father gave my grandmother a photo of her and my grandfather, taken just after they were married. In it he is tall and fair, handsomely Aryan, she is small and exotic, a beautiful Jewess. They were both brought up Catholic. The photo was taken in Prague, shortly before the war. My grandparents look very young, and gorgeous like film stars.

When my grandmother sees the photo, which my father has put into a beautiful frame to give to her, she begins crying once again. She is comforted by her friends, people whose names I have heard all my life, but have scarcely met. They soothe her in Czech, a language I do not understand.

Sometimes the pictures of the past are from documentaries. Like pictures from the Holocaust, those multitudes in concentration camps, eyes huge in their skulls, heads shaved, their skeletons too, too visible. My grandmother was also one of those haunted people.

*

Before I begin this story I go to visit my Jewish grand-mother in Melbourne. The curtains in her house are drawn against the heat that sings outside. I love the smell of her kitchen, so unlike an Australian kitchen. When I went to Czechoslovakia the kitchens had the same smell. I wonder how, when you are fleeing persecution to make a new life on the other side of the world, you pack the smell of the kitchen.

We drink iced water and I look around at the things that have always been there. The silk rug on the wall, the clock on the television that has a glass back through which you can see all its workings, the cushions of a koala and a kangaroo in muted fifties tones that she tapestried when they first arrived. She and I have never talked about the war, and I would not know how to bring the subject up. It is difficult enough to talk about simple things now that she is going deaf and her English is not as good as it was. I try to speak slowly, but my voice speeds up when I have to say things over and over. My grandmother shakes her head sadly because she doesn't understand what I am saying and this is just when I am saying something about the heat. I cannot imagine trying to talk about the war.

My grandmother's entire family was killed in concen-tration camps during the war. So many people—parents, grandparents, siblings, cousins, uncles, aunts. It's not an unfamiliar story. One just says, 'They were all killed', as if it is a simple matter. An undifferentiated subset of the larger undifferentiated subset of the six million Jews who perished in the Holocaust, people denied their chance to make great works of art or bring up families or work in the post office. What difference does it make that they were my relatives?

My grandmother married my grandfather when she was nineteen and he was twenty-one. He was a salesman, she was a secretary at the place where he worked. This is the story I have heard: when the Germans invaded Czechoslovakia a few years later, they said to my grandfather, 'Divorce your wife and we will take her and your sons away for a while and then when we have won the war you will all be reunited.' My grandfather refused. I don't know if he also said angrily, 'Do you think I am a complete fool?' or if perhaps he did try to believe them because that would be so much easier, and surely it couldn't be what he suspected, because that would be pure evil and human beings do not act that way to other human beings.

I don't know how many times my grandparents wondered just how brave they could be.

Where there are things not talked about much, family stories are a game of Chinese whispers. I do not know if the stories I have in my head are really what happened or a distillation of word vapours that fall one day like this, another like that. Nearly everything I think I know about my father's family, I heard from my mother, a fourth-generation Australian, who was told them over time by my father, who witnessed some, listened to others.

Because my grandfather would not divorce my grandmother, the Nazis took him away to a work camp in Poland where he worked hard alongside other enemies of the Nazis. This meant my grandmother got to stay in Prague for a while longer. She stayed with her two boys, my father and my uncle, with my grandfather's mother in her apartment.

It was my mother who told me that my grandmother was Jewish. I was about ten and it was a time when kids were calling other kids 'Jews' if they wouldn't give them things, and would yell 'Jew Jump' as they threw a lolly in the air for everyone to dive for. She explained who the Jews were, and talked about my grandmother and the war and threw in *The Merchant of Venice*. Years later she told me that Dad was angry that she had told us. 'He didn't want you to know, in case it all happened again, here in Australia.' The fewer people who know your blood, the harder it is to trace.

It used to seem silly to me that my father might worry about this. It used to seem impossible that such racial hatred and genocide would ever be part of the world again.

By the time the Nazis rounded my grandmother up, it was nearly the end of the war and they no longer bothered with the children. All the adult Jews left in Prague were called up for yet another census, and when they got there they realised they were to be taken away. Somehow my grandmother got word out about what was happening, and my great-grandmother packed a suitcase for her. My father took it to her. Because he was Jewish, he wasn't allowed to go on public transport so he had to drag the suitcase through the streets as best he could, wearing his yellow star. He was seven years old.

He told us this story one night after dinner. He cried as he told it. My mother said, 'You've never told me this. I've never heard this before.'

I don't know what was in the suitcase. I don't know what you'd put in a suitcase for someone to take to a concentration camp. Nothing you put in could possibly be enough.

*

Once when my brothers and I were much younger, my littlest brother told a joke about Hitler. The *Führer* was inspecting the troops and one of them sneezed. 'Who sneezed?' Hitler demands. No one answers so he orders the first row of soldiers to be shot. Then he asks again, louder, more aggressively, 'Who sneezed?' and still no one answers so Hitler orders the next row of soldiers to be shot and so on and so on, until there is only one soldier left. And Hitler—really loud and really angry by now—repeats, 'Who sneezed?' and the last soldier replies, 'I did,' and Hitler says, 'Aah, *Gesundheit.*'

It's a beautiful summer day and we're sitting outside under the walnut tree at my grandparents' place and my baby brother tells this joke. He is very cute pretending to be an angry Hitler. Not that he even knows who Hitler is, and I'm not entirely sure either, but he dissolves into giggles like he always does when he tells a joke. All the adults are completely silent for a while and I know that something has gone wrong. Then they start talking about something else, and in the car on the way home Mum and Dad tell us about the war. We're not really in trouble, us kids, except we sort of are, and I'm not sure why except that it's got to do with not being careful enough.

The garden my grandparents planted when they came to Australia had a row of roses along the front fence, a prickly pear by the front door and a backyard full of trees—walnut and almond, apricot and peach, lemon trees and grape vines. Always my grandparents would bring us fruit and nuts in season, although gradually all the trees died of old age, except the lemons. They planted a she-oak in the front garden, never believing it would grow to twenty metres high, but it did, and it flowers spectacularly.

My grandmother was liberated by the Allies only days before she would have been gassed. I think that her only brother was accidentally shot by the Allies, shortly after he had sent her word that she must escape or she would perish. I have seen a photograph of him, and he too is beautiful as though he has stepped from a film. I picture his death as a scene from a film, with him running for his life and then the shot ringing out, the force of the bullet thrusting his body forward, his arms reaching to the sky in anguish, before he falls to the ground. But it may not have happened anything like this.

There are lots of pieces missing from the story. I do not know anything about how my grandmother, my grand-father, my uncle and my father were reunited. I do not know if they recognised each other straightaway, or stood warily like strangers, hollow-eyed and fearful, unable to believe it was over.

I do not know how long all this would take to leave your waking life, and then how long before it left your dreaming and let you go to sleep without fear again.

*

Under Jewish law, my father is Jewish and my brothers and I are not, because my mother isn't. Under Nazi law we would never have been born. We were blue-eyed, very blond children, exactly the sort of children Hitler wanted.

I go to the theatre with my parents and during the

interval I tell my father that I am going to write this story. I tell him I want to talk to my grandmother about it. In a way I suppose I want his permission, I want him to tell me if it isn't a good idea.

'What is it you want to know?' asks my father. I'm not really sure. It is hard to talk about a story you haven't yet written, to frame questions about silences. It's like having someone test your hearing by asking you to tell them what you don't hear. Maybe it's that I want her to make the story for me—me scribbling it down as she speaks, my hand racing across the page to keep up with the pouring words.

The play we are seeing is an acclaimed overseas production of *Waiting for Godot*. For the entire first half there is a fault in a speaker in the theatre and static keeps bursting out. It is especially loud during the silences. Whenever there is a long pause in the dialogue, the theatre fills with a noise like flat applause or dull oceans. It makes us distracted and irritable, this static interference when we are supposed to hear silence.

'Let me tell you this,' says my father as we are going back into the theatre. 'Before the Nazis came, your grandmother felt no different to any other young woman in Prague.'

My father seems very formal when he says this, suddenly very European in the way of people who have been away a long time and think this is how the old country still is.

He says he will mention it to my grandmother, but when I visit I can tell that nothing has been said. I say nothing too.

When I went to Prague I stayed with an old friend of

my grandparents. He took me on long long walks through the streets of Prague and he showed me the places where my father and his family lived, schools my father went to, places my grandparents went dancing. He doesn't talk about the war either but he tells me how he wept the day my grandparents and the boys left to come to Australia. I peer up at window-panes glinting in the sun looking for traces of them, for glimpses of past ghosts waving to me or ducking back behind the curtains.

*

On the wall of the bedroom my grandmother has now, there is a drawing by me of a woman sewing patches together, sew, sew, sew until in the final frame she has made a patchwork hang-glider and is flying away. Fly, fly, fly. My grandmother has always sewn and knitted and made things, and I thought of her when I was drawing the picture. She loved it so much I had to give it to her. In a letter she wrote to say thank you, she said that all her life she has dreamed of being able to fly. When she was a girl, she could never go past a swing without getting on it to swing as high in the air as she could, to feel like she might almost be flying.

Chronicle 1—
The Massage

Sandra Goldbloom

For HG

Sandra Goldbloom is a Melbourne-based writer. Several of her short stories have been published in anthologies and journals. The Book of Rachel, *her first novel, is published by Allen & Unwin.*

HE IS IN HOSPITAL again.

Seated on the end of the bed, I contemplate his feet. Dry, scaly, the ankles uncharacteristically bloated. Thorny little spikes of skin poke out at wild angles from around the edges of his heels. His long big toe puts me in mind of a sadsack character in a children's story book. Toe Man. Sad old Toe Man.

I take his foot and cradle it between my warm hands.

'Cold,' I remark, repelled by the thick, chilly flesh. His leg is a dead weight. I release his foot.

'They're always cold. No circulation. Ever since the surgery.'

I do not enquire which occasion: it is unlikely we will agree. We would become irritated with each other. Eventually we would bicker.

In the past six years, there have been many surgeries. Many. At first they were performed as couplets: angioplasty—two; removal of gangrene—two; prostate cancer—two. More recently, a triple bypass, followed ten days later by a single heart attack. 'His first', was how the medical staff put it at the time.

Excision of—

Sometimes I imagine he will leave us by stealth, disappeared, one small body part at a time.

*

The cuffs of his pyjamas have come to rest—or are they hitched up?—midway down his calf muscles, which have grown slack.

He is miserable today. I would like to cheer him up. I would like—as ever—to please him.

'Would you like me to massage your feet?'

His swift response does not surprise me, not in the least.

'Yes please.' Immediately he begins wriggling himself into a position of greater comfort. 'That would be nice.' He clears his throat.

'You know,' he begins, ordering his thoughts as though he were about to recount the story for the first time, 'when I travelled I had many different sorts of massage...'

*

A list of foreign capitals is rattled off, large towns are named, and the variations on the massage theme he experienced in them: on tables, futons, mats. (He never mentions beds, which does not stop me from wondering.) With the passing of time it has become more difficult for him to recollect precisely. Berlin for—? What was it in Berlin? In Rome, a woman—or was it a man? Prague? Ah, Prague. He sighs wistfully but doesn't elaborate. Leningrad? Ah yes, Leningrad—in Leningrad, he recalls, there was rigour. Oy, how his flesh was pummelled! He smiles—then worries the inside corner of his lower lip with his incisors. Or was that Barcelona? He stops chewing his lip. No, he is adamant: Leningrad. A man from Barbados in London. Hanoi—hmm, light, feathery hands in Hanoi. Cups! he exclaims. Bamboo cups in Shanghai. He enjoyed the cups. In Haifa: chop, chop, chop, chop. Rapid, strong, rhythmic. No, he pauses, now that I think of it, the chopping may have been—

He purses his lips and frowns. A small, frustrated frown.

*

Listening—and not listening—to the Muzak of his voice as he meanders the world, I consider, once again, the colours in the ward.

They are bland. Nothing about them excites the senses. Pale. Everything pale: pink walls, beige vinyl , white sheets and curtains, pastel cotton blankets. Even his pyjamas are pale. Faded powder-blue. His favourite pair of faded powder-blue pyjamas.

There is a stool, a modern ottoman. Its frame is made of tubular steel, the seat of pale grey leather. (Is it leather, or one of those clever vinyls?) Two commercial prints— bucolic in theme—hang on one wall: unimaginative works, they are rendered drearier still by the insipid colours depicting—where? Australia?

My clothes are black, my lipstick earthy red. And there, on the bench opposite his bed, a cut-glass vase filled with freesias as yellow as ripe corn.

A bronze Christ, twice crucified—once to the cross, once to the wall—hangs above his bald, Jewish head. The son of God appears to be listening intensely, leaning forward, head to one side, as if attempting to catch every word of this yarn about international rubbings and unguents.

*

Papa's reminiscences have become tiresome. In Milan, I release his foot, turn from him, and walk to the mirror. I watch my lips shape his words, as I mouth the intact fragments of his memories with him, grateful that he pays me no heed. That he is unable to see me. From bed to mirror, our angles do not converge.

The pouches under my eyes seem more puffy than usual. While he continues his journey, massage by massage, I indulge my vanity.

I exert a gentle pressure beneath my left eye, moving my index finger along the bloated curve, slowly, a few millimetres at a time, until a full arc is completed. The touch of my fingers feels cool against the overheated skin of my face. In the background his voice continues, fluttering, a sea breeze rippling through muslin curtains.

'... even had a woman walk all over my back once. Imagine that!'

At last! There it is. The ending he so loves. He chuckles quietly. Years after the event—could it be twenty? twenty years?—it continues to produce a boyish wonder in him, though at which particular aspect I have never known. That he had the audacity to permit such an act?

'Now, where was that? Singapore? No, I think that one must have been Kyoto.'

'You always said it was Tokyo, Papa.'

I turn from my haggard reflection and face him, just in time to see him cock an eyebrow. A little testily—only a little; we are on good behaviour with each other today— a little testily he says:

'Well then, it must have been Tokyo.'

Satisfied, he settles into the bank of pillows and offers me his feet.

'Left first, or right?'

'Let's start on the right foot, Papa.'

*

Each element proves to be in perfect harmony with the other: my body seated on the ottoman with the height of the bed, the location of Papa's foot on the mattress with my hands and arms. Everything. No adjustments need be made.

A white towel is draped across my lap. While Papa makes himself comfortable, I rub my hand back and forth over the cotton, enjoying the coarse, luxuriant pile, and find myself wishing for towels like these for my own bath-room. But this texture of towelling seems only to be found in hospital wards.

Papa gives a cheeky little hitch to his pyjamas. I smile at this, and at the silver wisps of what remains of his hair fanned out on the pillow, which gives him a soft, angelic appearance. Elderly angel.

He folds his hands one over the other and rests them on his stomach. Unsatisfied with this arrangement, he straightens his arms and places them alongside his body. Then he closes his eyes and releases a tremulous, anticipatory quiver of breath. Papa is ready for his Australian massage to begin.

He looks to me to be laid out.

From a pump-action plastic bottle, I squeeze out a large dollop of moisturising cream and smear it from one hand to the other. Above his pallid—no, white, no, I must say it, above the naked...the greyish...the deathlike-white skin of his long legs, my hands, browned by the sun, divested of jewellery, are poised, hovering. Hovering.

In that moment my hands appear to me as birds, indecisive creatures, trembling with uncertainty. To go on, or fly off? Withdraw or stay? My cheeks burn; my skin begins to itch. My heart is racing.

Hovering hands, racing heart.

I wonder—cannot help wondering—if Papa is aware of it, this moment in which I have become afraid of what I have offered. But for the shallow rise and fall of his chest, he does not move. Not so much as an eyelash, not one nervous twitch. He is in a state of serene anticipation. I imagine that if he notices anything at all it is that I have not yet begun.

Does he feel the electric current in the air? Does he feel—as I do—a twinge of...what?...Impropriety? Yes, that's it. Impropriety. A certain lack of decency, to be massaging my father's feet. Indecent to be running my hands over his flesh. A transgression.

Hands hovering. Heart racing.

Too late now to withdraw. How could I possibly explain? 'Sorry, Papa. I've changed my mind. To touch you like this is too unfamiliar. And too familiar.' Hardly. Whatever I said, it would embarrass us both.

*

I avert my eyes, fixing on a space on the wall—above his head and away from the suffering Christ. I work by feeling out the landscape, spreading a thick layer of cream over his foot and ankle. Stroke. Knead. Slide. Press. Around. Up. Down. Brisk and functional movements. Short, tentative strokes. More gingerly, I work over his leg, saved from any impropriety—from further impropriety—by the cuffs of his pyjamas. He twitches slightly when I slip my fingers between his long, dry toes. I feel an urge to tickle his sole. Promptly, and with decorum, the urge is repressed.

*

The moment has come to abandon the security of the wall. I need to pump more cream from the bottle. Looking at him is unavoidable. Besides, I'm curious.

His eyes are still closed. It is safe to peer at him. The length of him, from his face, along his body to his legs and feet.

All that is visible of the thick coating of cream is a sheen; his foot, his shin, his slack calf, all are glistening with it.

Papa's breath is even. Is he asleep? Seeing him so utterly at peace, something shifts in me; a physical sensation.

What a commonplace, to speak of a weight being lifted from the shoulders, yet, extraordinarily, that's precisely what I feel. There are no other words. My spine straightens, the knots in my shoulders and neck dissolve. I have become light-headed. Is this how compassion feels? Light, and suffused with love? With forgiveness? I smile at him.

Papa. My hero and my nemesis. How desperately I wanted his approval.

*

I have always thought of him as a powerful figure, a robust, passionate man who would never be damaged, who would never become ill. Who would never die.

Never die? Well, not never. Never is inaccurate. He would die. Of course he would die. But later. Not this year, not next. Or the next. Later. Much later. One day. Isn't that always his little joke? 'I don't have time to die', he says. 'There's too much I want to do yet. Still too much to see. There's a world out there that needs saving. No time to die. I shall live to be one hundred and twenty.'

Biz ahindert un tzvuntzig.

Just like Moses.

*

I sit on the ottoman, holding his foot in my cream-soaked hands. Along his shins, against the pallor of whiteness, the finest of red and blue lines stand out—veins and arteries, and dense galaxies of reddish-purple where blood vessels have burst. His shins resemble a section of electronic wiring. Intricate. Delicate. A fatherboard. Or are they the detail of a Jackson Pollock? 'Number 9'? 'Number 43'? If I could paint, I would make art of his red and blue veins, his purple patches, set against the canvas of his white skin.

Perhaps start a movement. Gather in all those women who wish to draw the remaining parts of their aged fathers: skin, veins and arteries, limbs, balding heads, the signifying scars where organs and protuberances have been removed. Forlorn Toe Men.

Papaism.

*

Maintaining a gentle hold on Toe Man, I walk around to the other side of the bed. I know a thing or two about massage myself: don't release the subject, maintain the energy flow.

Do not let go.

'Just changing sides, Papa,' I whisper.

He smiles and murmurs, 'Mmm.'

I am not going away, not deserting him.

*

I put my weight behind my arms and give them power. Movement becomes uninhibited. Fluid. Sweep upwards, slide down, more pressure here, less there. Long, soothing strokes. Their soothing touches me, too.

The prickly tacks of skin soften and lie down, the sandpaper rasp grows silky. Blood begins to circulate. Colour returns to his feet; their pinkness is childlike.

Beads of perspiration form on my upper lip; I lick them away. Without haste, so as not to disturb the rhythm, I lift my right arm to my forehead and use the sleeve of my blouse to brush away the sweat that has gathered there while I continue the flow of the massage with the left. He is patient. Patient.

*

Three-quarters of an hour passes. I draw my hands down his leg, past his ankles to his toes and out into the air.

Soaring birds of hands. Soaring birds. Out into the air.

*

'Did you enjoy that?'

'Mmm, I did.' His speech is thick. 'Very much.' He pauses. 'Thank you.'

I have pleased him.

'Would you like me to come again tomorrow?'

He places an upturned hand on the bedclothes, an invitation to me to hold it. I hold it. His hand feels dry. Dry and flaky. He wraps those elegant fingers around my hand, draws my hand to his lips, kisses my fingers.

He nods. 'That would be lovely.'

We smile at each other.

'Goodbye then, Papa. See you tomorrow.'

I am almost out the door when I turn to look at him. In all likelihood his eyes have not left me.

'I love you, Papa.'

Quietly, I leave the room.

The Fiftieth Gate

Mark Baker

Mark Raphael Baker lectures in Modern Jewish History at the University of Melbourne. He received his doctorate from Oxford University and is the editor of Generation, *a quarterly magazine of Australian Jewish thought, art and culture.*

His book, The Fiftieth Gate: A Journey Through Memory, *won a NSW Premier's award and received a high commendation by the Fellowship of Australian Writers/Christina Stead Award. It was voted Audio Book of the Year by the Braille and Talking Book Library Awards and has been on a number of shortlists including the Victorian Premier's Award, South Australian Premier's Award,* Age *Book of the Year, National Biography Award and NSW Premier's History Awards.*

He is currently completing a novel, a mystical thriller about faith set in an ultra-Orthodox Jewish community.

Mark lives in Melbourne with his wife and three children.

here in this carload
i am Hinda
tell him that i…

THE GHETTO POLICEMAN slams the door, pushing
the darkness of night into our vehicle. There are three windows on either side of the carriage, but the light outside is
insufficient to illuminate the box. Not a box, I think, but a
coffin. My prayers and hands reach out for my children.

'Yenta! Martale!'

My pleas are answered by a woman whose body leans
against mine, begging for a cup of water. 'My child,' she
pleads. I pass her the single flask preserved for my family.
She pours water into the mouth of her infant, at rest in her
arms. Shadowy figures grope in the dark, forming a sea of
human pillars held upright in a wooden cage.

'We must change carriages,' I protest, 'no air in here,
can't breathe.'

When I last used the train from the Kolejowa railway
station, a Polish officer sitting behind a square window had
obliged me with a numbered ticket. His face, cut in half by
a bushy moustache, nodded in the direction of a glimmer-
ing train.

'Radom,' he said.

'Please, let me come,' my daughters had begged, but I sent them to school, reassuring them with promises of future trips with their father who frequently travelled to Częstochowa to collect glassware. That was in 1939, eleven months before the truck collected Leib from his cell in Starachowice.

'Jews, we're finished,' someone matter-of-factly comments. Everyone is waiting as the train signals its departure with a shrill whistle, as if it were a prompt for the passengers to begin reciting the mourner's *Kaddish*:

'*Yisgadal ve yiskadash shmei rabba.*'

'Quiet,' a woman shouts, 'they won't kill young people.'

Her futile protest increases the volume of those sanctifying God's name, inciting her to scream wildly, cursing.

'Cowards! Bless life, not death. They're taking us to work.'

A child's voice rises defiantly above the rest: 'Blessed be the Lord who has kept us alive, sustained us, and brought us to this day.'

'Yenta, not here, not in this box.'

'Mameh,' she answers, but her voice is drowned out by a chorus of wails.

A man lies prostrate as if in prayer. He is pushing his head against the floorboards.

'Breathe through the floor,' I call out to my children.

People struggle to curl their body to the floor, pushing at the person pressed against them so that human bodies are flying over the shoulders of the strong ones, like chicken wings strewn on a plate. A young boy is shouting for his mother as his head rubs against the ceiling of the train, until it falls back limply. My own foot knocks against a head. I strain to lift it but it is trapped beneath the weight of sleeping passengers. A man is folded on the floor like a pair of ironed trousers. The screams are indistinguishable; every voice sounds like the cry of my daughters, but there is no way of knowing.

I bury my face into a woollen jacket which brushes against my eyes. I crouch in this position for an unmeasured distance, counting time by the steady motion of the train wheels speeding across tracks on unknown terrain. 'Martale, Yentale,' I whisper. There is silence on the train save for the sound of a tortured wheeze. The air is mixed with the pungent odour of fresh vomit and faeces. It is an effort to breathe, but I strain my neck to the edge of the woollen torso and inhale. We stand like a forest of trees. My fingers form a web against the wooden beams of the ceiling. My head spins with the terror of losing my daughters.

They are lost somewhere in this monster with infinite hands and limbs, perhaps swallowed in its jaws. I rest this way through the night. Sweat drips from my cheeks into the void below. Behind my eyes are dancing images in shades of grey and black. I imagine they are the shadows of Yenta and Marta. Their tiny heads and plaited hair rest easily, lulled into dreams by Yiddish melodies which tell of Daddy's return and handsome grooms. *Ay li lu*, my lips quaver, *lu li lu*. The songs reach the ears of Baruch and Yossl as they march up the hill where work-papers will surely secure their survival. For my Leibush, it is too late.

Prayers float across the carriage.

'*Sha.*'

'*Mameh, vi bistu*, where are you?'

It is Marta. Please, I beg, let her through, but there is no possibility of movement through the parched forest grown in this box. The silence has surrendered to a rising wail, joined by my own voice. The scramble for air starts again; elbows push against wrinkled faces, squeezing bodies onto the floor. A mother screams that her baby is dead, singing to its broken innocence until she throws it beneath her feet. Silver spoons, faded photographs and feathers fly overhead, the emptied contents of a case abandoned by its owner. A young child has pulled his clothes off; mortified, he claws his neck with bloodied fingernails. I recognise his green shirt from a familiar image of hanging cloth flapping from our neighbour's window alongside the fringes of a ritual shawl. Yenta was wearing a blouse and yellow skirt: I scour the ground for flashes of colour.

'Water, water,' a man desperately shouts through a half-open window. He is suspended on the hind of a sleeping child when the train accelerates, before slowing down to accomplish a sharp bend. I recognise the man from the bakery in Pilsudski Street, his head rummaging inside an oven from where he produces poppyseed cakes balanced on a rack. Now his head is poking through a window and with a single thrust forward I watch his body slide into an open gap. A shoe drops onto a child. Within seconds the train pulls to a halt, and from outside can be heard the commotion of slamming doors and soldiers screaming orders to each other in German, followed by gunshots whose blasting sounds reverberate in the sky.

The train restores its winding motion through mountainous terrain. Passengers huddle with their hands stretched upward. A moving shadow tugs at my skirt.

'Yenta,' I instinctively mutter, but my hands cannot identify the silent form tied to my legs. We hang together like
this for a prolonged period, measuring time by raspy
breaths and the churning of wheels. Through a part of the
window I see the tips of pine trees framed like a moving
picture. A new rumour ripples through the train:

'Have you heard of Obermajdan? They say that is
where we are headed.'

The train comes to a standstill. Railway workers
approach the carriage. People near the window hang their
hands out begging for water. The thirst is harder to bear
than the hunger; a desperate woman feeds her baby its own
urine, while another offers a child the salty juice of her skin
to lick. A man stands on the platform, his face and skeletal
eyes looking upward toward an invisible spot. He raises a
hand toward his neck, and flicks a finger across his throat.

The doors are drawn open by gloved hands brandish-
ing whips. I close my eyes against the rush of light. We fall
onto the platform in a continuous wave. I step over the
body of an old man who has collapsed at the foot of the
train, as if it were prey for vultures to eat. Piles of clothes
form soft mountains on the ground, alongside hills of shav-
ing brushes and a lake shimmering with assorted shapes of
eye-glasses. 'Why do these people not take care of their
belongings?' I wonder. A new pile forms, composed of
fatigued bodies dragged from one of twenty carriages running the length of the railway siding. The bodies have
horribly bloated bellies and the surface of their skin is
already marked with sores. My eyes involuntarily gaze at
fallen bits and pieces: legs, arms, torsos and heads which I
recognise from flashing fragments of my life; from tables

adorned with Sabbath linen and flames lit by mothers blessing flickering lights; from children licking fingers in Mama's shop and fathers sewing suits with skilful hands; from swaying shapes draped in white offering prayers in synagogues consumed by flames on sacred days. 'Yenta,' I scream, and I hear the echo of a cry calling *Mameh* bursting from the depth of the heap.

'Mameh,' Marta shouts.

A guard grips her arm and drives her into the loose crowd. I race toward her and embrace my daughter before a whip separates us.

'Water,' she whimpers. There is none to offer.

In the distance I hear the sound of an orchestra playing a military tune.

'Martale, look. A train station. Look, ticket-windows, and over there. A baggage counter.'

My clothes smell of decay and ruin, yet the music revives my body. It makes me feel human again. The orchestra members appear, marked by yellow stars, under a clock face whose hands read 10.25. A new sense of order reigns above the chaos of milling people, comforting me in the face of this unknown transit point. A man dressed in a railway uniform asks for our tickets, and conducts us to a small square, as if we are travellers on a spring holiday.

'Gold, cash, foreign currency and jewellery must be turned in at the ticket office,' a voice blasts above the din. 'You will be given receipts for these valuables. Your valuables will be returned to you later on presentation of your receipts.'

Signs, in Polish and German, point in all directions.

'*Station Obermajdan! Umsteigen nach Bialystok und Wolkowysk.*'

'Obermajdan Station! Change here for Bialystok and Wolkowysk.'

The music beckons us towards the continuation of our journey. A mother scolds her child for soiling his pants; a young girl combs her hair as if preparing for a date; a father begs his friend for money to purchase a ticket to join his cousins in Bialystok. My eyes follow the railway lines, wondering where their tracks will lead us. Who knows how long it has been since we linked ourselves with these lines near my house? A young girl behind us tightens her scarf, an old woman sits on her suitcase. They are all waiting, but the railway lines lead nowhere. Was the music also a figment of my imagination? And what is this huge wall covered with yellowing branches leading off from the square?

'The tickets,' I shout at Marta. 'Come, let's ask that man in the railway uniform where we can purchase tickets for Warsaw.'

My eyes search for the uniformed man but settle on barbed wire fences. Another train pulls up on the other side. Those alive pour out as if a flood of water has been unleashed from its ramparts. The languages mix in the air: Polish, German, Yiddish, all lost in shrill sounds whose elements I cannot decipher. Bent figures stream out with suitcases and bags, dressed in warm fur coats. I feel jealousy towards them, for they have retained the possessions we relinquished at the start of the war.

'Water,' they beg. '*Vasser, vasser.*'

A man draws a cup from his coat pocket. Before he has

time to bring it to his lips a boy sinks his teeth into his arm and catches the falling container.

An officer dressed in black begins to address us on the square where we have collected. He invites us to leave our baggage and to move forward toward the baths. We are instructed to take our identification papers, any valuable objects and the few toiletries brought with us.

'Should we take our towels?' Marta asks me. I shake my head; all our belongings have been left on the train.

'Where is Yentale?' she inquires.

I shake my head again as we walk through the en-closure set against a wall of barbed wire. It is overgrown with branches and thick green leaves. The music plays for us as we follow the trail past a muddied ditch. Ahead I can make out the shape of watchtowers. I glance behind and notice the workers with sky blue armbands unpacking our baskets and cases. Perhaps they will find my small brown case and retrieve its contents: a spare dress, an outfit for each of the girls, a pouch containing money gathered at the last moment, and a picture of Leib staring into the camera with his arms wrapped around his four children.

We arrive at another square where a large shed stands before us. I manage to cast a glance inside before I am pushed on by a whip which drives the crowd to quicken its pace. The image lingers: a mountain of clothes, and in another window, shoes, enough to clothe the whole of Starachowice.

A whip cracks to signal the command: '*Achtung!* Men will stay where they are. Women and children will undress in the shed to the left.'

The command is repeated: 'Men to the right! Women and children to the left.'

Near us a young girl, about Yenta's age, says goodbye to her father, and stroking his eyes, comforts him: 'Have no fear, Daddy. Daddy, don't worry,' and then she hands over her watch, saying: 'Take it. You'll remain alive and you'll have it. Take it.'

'Women and children will remove shoes before entering. Children's socks must be placed in their shoes, sandals or boots.'

We enter a wooden barrack where I follow the movements of other women. First I remove my shoes and tie them together with special laces passed around by inmates. I help Marta remove her tiny black shoes. She ties the shoes together on her own. I fold my black coat on a bench, and place the remainder of my clothes in a neat pile: a white blouse, grey skirt, and thin stockings. I hesitate to remove my underwear, shamed by my own nakedness before women whose homes I have visited clad in Sabbath finery and a silk kerchief. Marta stares at my bareness, while I admire her body which is flowering in its graceful prime. We move silently through the door toward the next shed like brides headed for ritual purification.

This room is lined by female inmates who shear our hair. I wait my turn, and diffidently watch my dark mane fall, as if it were cut from a captive animal. Women cooperatively hand over their wigs, the last vestige of their modesty.

'A little shorter here please,' Marta tells the hairdresser. 'Please, make it even.'

Her thick black hair drops in a single lock like a

twisted potato peel. 'What's going to happen to us?' she asks the barber, who flinches before gliding the clippers across her bowed head.

'*Schneller. Schneller. Schneller.*'

I feel shame in front of the male officers who flick their whips in our direction, forcing us to run until we are arranged like a military detachment of pink flesh.

'Faster, faster.'

I hold Marta by her fragile arms. Her pace is flagging.

'Hands above heads.'

'Marta,' I scream, 'Stay with Mameh.' We thrust our hands into the air as commanded, and quicken our frenzied pace. A terrible odour wafts past my nose, different from the smell of decay which dominated our carriage.

'*Schneller. Schneller.*'

Marta is dancing, reaching with her fingertips for the dark clouds. Her shaved crown glistens under the sky which closes above us as we run into a narrow passage bordered with flowers and a pine grove. Three musicians play a flute, violin and mandolin under a tree at the entrance to the tube. They perform a harmonious dirge. I recognise it as the nightly lullaby my mother sang as she stroked my hair until my eyes would close in sleep. '*Ay li lu,*' I hum to Marta. Her hands are performing lyrical movements in the air.

'Faster, faster,' the policemen in black uniform order. 'The bath water is going to get cold. Hurry hurry.'

'*Ay li lu.*'

Naked men have joined the crowd; a child runs into the arms of her father. Ahead of us, an SS officer beats an elderly woman with his club for delaying the line. He turns toward a young child, no more than four years old, and tears her from her mother's arms. He raises the infant above his head like a sporting trophy and throws her onto the ground. She does not move. I am careful to step over her body when I pass, bending down to touch her warm hand.

The narrow path suddenly breaks open to reveal another square occupied by a concrete building. It resembles a temple from ancient times. Its entrance is decorated by wooden ornamental vases planted along a row of flower beds. A Star of David is etched into the gable on the front wall of the building. The doors are screened by a dark curtain bearing the Hebrew inscription: 'This is the gate of God through which the righteous shall enter.'

'Mameh,' Martale whispers. 'It's a *shul*. They want us to pray.'

I press her close to my body as we ascend five cement steps. Police dogs bark at the rising throng. From the side of the building I notice a bulldozer moving huge piles of yellow earth, leaving a cloud of dust in its wake. Teams of men are pushing tip-carts around the entrance. A tall man, with broad shoulders and black hair, cracks a thick whip at us. Another man, shorter and younger, bares his sword. We freeze in our steps, our arms still punching the air. One of the dogs is released and tears into the crowd, setting his teeth into the skin of a woman who shrieks in pain. Blood spurts onto my naked flesh. I emit a panicked cry, burying Marta into my bosom. Then another dog: 'Go, Bari,' I hear its commander shout, as if it was being sent to fetch a stick.

We are pushed through the gates of the temple leading into a dark narrow corridor. I hear the unmistakable sound of screams.

A door opens. I lift Marta, hugging her against my body.

'*Ay li lu.*'

We are pushed by the crowd into a square room whose walls are already lined with early arrivals. Families huddle in corners; a man covers his eyes in prayer; a girl stands in a puddle of water, kicking her own excrement. My eyes fixate on the baked-tile floor, sloping downward toward a platform.

'No more,' a woman screams.

'There's not space.'

Nickel-plated shower heads protrude from the ceiling. At least five hundred people have been piled into the room.

'No more.'

A child is thrown from the door above our heads.

'Mameh,' Marta whispers. 'Where is Yenta?'

'Sha, sha.' I stroke her bare head, hoping the caress will send her to sleep, but the deafening screams rise.

'*Yisgadal ve yiskadash shmei rabba.*'

Bodies are flying above us.

'*Shma yisrael.* Hear O Lord.'

The doors are closed and our eyes look upward at the shower heads, praying for a stream of water.

We have bonded again into a single shape, a fleshy creature with writhing heads, arms and legs, dancing in contortions.

Two dark eyes. Eyes, peering through holes on the other side of the door. The eyes close, and open again. Do they see my eyes? A cloudy ethereal haze envelops the room, heightening our cherubic romp before God's throne. The eyes dance too, in sockets staring through peepholes.

'*Ay li lu.*'

My heart pounds wildly. 'Mameh,' Marta hisses. 'I can't breathe. Where is the water?'

'God will breathe for you, my darling.'

A heavy weight compresses my chest. My head spins, blurring floor, ceiling, heads and limbs into a compact mass. A mother holds up her child to avoid the crush; it is Malka, the tailor's wife. She is wedged against her other child, his head drooping and arms stiffening like a broken doll.

Two eyes watch from glassy cavities behind the sealed door. What do they see?

Letters dancing, etched on broken tablets soaring up to angel arms tapping on the gate to God's palace.

Aleph, beit. Holy letters blue and bloated, befouled with filth and excrement.

Gimmel, daleth. Rivers of blood gushing through gates from the crowns of wounded scrolls. Letters with eyes, holes wide open, tangled in words carved on arms strapped in leather.

Heh, vav spewed from twisted tongues and mouths. Seraphs dancing for God, banging at His gate.

Zayin, het. Bulging eyes peering through keyholes broader than Wierzbnik. Stone letters turning locks; limp bodies lying in a room larger than the world.

Tet, yod. The point of light, pouring through the fiftieth gate.

tell him

tell Him that i

My Grandfathers' Graves

Tobsha Learner

Tobsha Learner was born in England and has lived in the UK, Australia and the US. She has worked extensively for stage, radio and film. Among her plays are the highly acclaimed Witchplay, Glass Mermaid, Wolf, SNAG *and* Seven Acts of Love as Witnessed by a Cat. *Her films include* Succubus *and* Antonio's Angel. *She is also the author of* Quiver *and* Madonna Mars. *She lives in Los Angeles and is currently working on a new collection of stories entitled* 'Tremble'.

I was born in England, grew up in London and have spent half my adult life in Australia. My mother was born in Israel, which then was known as Palestine, my father in England. My parents spent some of their childhood and early adulthood in Australia and then emigrated to England so that my father could pursue his doctorate. Neither family goes back further than one generation in England or Australia—and with such a huge amount of geographical displacement, the whole issue of cultural identity naturally permeates practically everything I do.

We were a family that celebrated both Passover and Christmas. My father, as a child of a socialist and then as a mathematician, was vehemently anti-religion and suspicious of anything too spiritual. My mother, the child of practising Jews, was given to bouts of belief and has always invested imaginatively in the spiritual and metaphysical world. We were brought up around friends of all hues and all religions and sexual persuasions, a great legacy and one that has influenced both my writing and my outlook. I have a strong abhorrence for any kind of ghetto and have been fortunate not to have experienced enough adversity to drive me into one...yet.

This was not the experience of much of my immediate family. My mother's father lost most of his family in the

Holocaust. Thus, as an unapologetic product of the diaspora and the child of secular intellectuals, I decided to write about two great influences in my childhood, two men of distinctly different Jewish heritages: my grandfathers.

England/Grandfather Bill

The first half of my life fell under the tutelage of my father's father, the English-born son of a Polish Jew. Bill Learner was born in Wardour Street, SoHo; the Jews spent time briefly in the West End before moving to the East End. After being born to Arnold and Tobsha Learner (my namesake) the family travelled to Newcastle-upon-Tyne, where my grandfather grew up under the heady influence of the local socialism and the mining rights movement. By the time he married Elsie, a local beauty and Protestant working-class girl, Bill was a Newtonian and a self-confessed atheist.

Bill, known as the Doc, had originally been named Abraham. Whether the abridged and completely unrelated name Bill was an attempt to assimilate, or whether it was my grandmother's anglicisation of a remote exoticism, is a mute point. The truth was that plain old Bill with his faint Northern accent was as English as you could get. The only remnants of his Jewish heritage as far as I can remember were his intellectualism, a fervent interest in chess and a passionate attention to the rights of the underdog—worker or otherwise. Diminutive, at five foot two, and fiercely intelligent, he was a man of little words who I totally idolised as a small child. I was the eldest of three and pretty ferocious myself.

When I was eight my parents separated, and my mother was always attempting to haul in the strong arm of the patriarch to apply some discipline. My grandfather, not my father, was still the ruling male of the clan. Even into his late sixties and seventies he radiated authority and a certain old-world canniness; a very British wisdom borne out of having had to work his way up through the class system.

In the late 1920s he had graduated as a doctor of chemistry and had been involved in the invention of plastic paint. He was also involved with demonstrating against Mosley. He was very close to his cousin Barney, who we knew as Uncle Barney and who was a huge bear of a man, the physical antithesis of my grandfather. Fiercely loyal to Bill, Grandad told stories of the two of them going after Mosley's fascists. He claimed the only thing a blackshirt understood was a knuckle sandwich. In retrospect I'm inclined to agree. During the war Bill ran a paint factory up in the north of England; as he was too old to fight, his contribution was the manufacture of war supplies. He did, however, belong to the home army and was responsible for planting a boy on the roof of his factory to watch for air raids. He was lucky—Elsie, his wife, lost her only brother, aged eighteen, on the beaches of Dunkirk.

In the late 1940s my grandfather brought his small family to Australia. While in Australia he settled down to a life of commerce, starting a business in Little Collins Street. My father was sent to Wesley and then to Melbourne University, and Grandad's socialism dwindled to the occasional visits to jail to teach prison inmates chess.

In early retirement and imbued with the kind of wanderlust and nostalgia emigration inflicts, he returned to

England a wealthy man. The family first settled in Bexhill-on-Sea, a tiny hamlet on the south-east coast, in a house that was way too large for three (by this time my aunt, twenty-one years younger than her brother, had been born). My grandfather spent his time studying the stock market and playing his first love, chess. I remember challenging him over a breakfast of toast and Robinson's marmalade; he would always beat me in five moves while reading the *Sunday Times*. I think I was about eight at the time, but even then I had a strong sense of injustice. My grandfather was a chess champion so my father always gave me a queen start, but somehow Bill couldn't bear losing to me. Perhaps he was making a point about life being inherently unfair.

Everywhere they moved to Grandad got heavily involved with the local chess club. They lived in Malta for a while and he founded the chess club there. It was his main social outlet, as both he and his wife became increasingly isolated.

In the 1970s they moved back to England into a large mock Tudor mansion in the seaside resort of Eastbourne. It is of them in this quaint sleepy town of boarding schools and repertory theatre companies that I have the most vivid memories: the hushed reverence with which we tiptoed around my grandfather asleep in his big leather armchair, 'The Two Ronnies' blaring away on the TV; the boiled sweets in the drawer; the tick-tock of the clock in the hallway, marking the ebbing away of life; celebrating Christmas with them every year with Bill in his Father Christmas costume of cottonwool beard and red paper hat, distributing presents from under the tree.

*

I have often wondered about Bill's rejection of all things spiritual, particularly in his last years. He always had a very antagonistic viewpoint on religion. His own parents had rejected some of the confines of their traditional Polish upbringing and, interestingly, all of Grandad's siblings married out, which must have been a radical departure in the 1920s. As a doctor of chemistry he came from the Newtonian, mechanistic school of thought. As far as he was concerned, there was no concrete evidence of God's existence, ergo he did not exist. Ironically, this staunch unwavering atheism gave no comfort to a life marred by tragedy. His own father, my great-grandfather Arnold, died young of pneumonia three months before the cure was found; my great aunt Sophie (the beloved baby of the family) died of breast cancer; and my father, Arnold, Bill's only son, was killed in a road accident at the age of forty.

How my grandfather survived emotionally is a mystery. He certainly had no solace in faith. I remember him telling me just after my father was killed, when I was sixteen, that my father was gone, that he was no more than dead flesh and that the pain was now with the living. This brutal observation undoubtedly came from a place of great pain; Arnold had been his pride and joy. I can only assume that Grandad was trying to jolt me into some concrete comprehension of my father's sudden death. But for me it was a harsh, unforgiving black and white view of the world, reducing it to a primordial amoral struggle for survival.

I could not then, and still can't, accept that destiny could ever be so arbitrary and my natural inclination was to create meaning where perhaps there wasn't any. For me this is to be human, but Grandad came from a different world. He'd grown up around a society crippled by class and religion, and I think he saw an investment in the spiritual as disempowering, an abdication of responsibility. He fiercely believed in the nurture over nature argument and that, given educational opportunity, the pauper could become a prince. He himself had overcome economic hardships and had won scholarships and achieved educationally, becoming a highly successful businessman despite his socialism.

Bill and Elsie lived only a few years after my father's sudden death, their spirits broken. Elsie, who was nine years younger than Bill, died unexpectedly one English winter, and Grandad died of grief months later. I had migrated to Australia by that time and despite our pleas they had never returned again for a visit. I don't even know where Bill is buried.

Australia/Josef Moses

Somewhere in the family albums is a series of photos of Josef, my maternal grandfather, standing by his tombstone, his arm stretched over the austere but impressive granite block and a proud smile playing across his aquiline features. It's a defiant fist to mortality. When asked, he would always say: 'I'm not going to wait for the grave, the grave can wait for me.' On several occasions at various Jewish functions a distant friend would approach my mother and express their sympathies at his passing, not understanding that the grave was lying there, empty and waiting...

If you looked closer at the photo you'd see that under my grandfather's Hebrew name are a series of names etched into the stone. These are the names of those who had no grave: his father's name, an eight-year-old brother, nearly all of his cousins, aunts, uncles, over a hundred people who had perished with the six million. The grave was Josef's piece of land, his final resting place in his final country. But it was also a memorial to a family whose ancient cemetery, in a small *shtetl* on the other side of the world, had been wiped out of existence by the Nazis in the hope that no one would remember the unburied.

One hot afternoon in Bondi, in Josef's tiny but immaculate flat which was crowded with 1950s furniture, a huge colour TV, photos of births, bar mitzvahs and weddings, posters of Israel pinned over the kitchen stove, the perpetual smell of chicken soup and something slightly sour underneath, he sat me down and made me record his life on tape. I was a restless twenty-four-year-old and slightly resentful of the fact that I had been anointed official family historian by my mother because of my then budding playwriting skills.

I learned about my Russian and Polish grandparents only upon my emigration to Australia at the age of nineteen, when I was old enough to be curious about a heritage that I had very little knowledge of and naive enough to think it sounded exotic.

Josef Moses Rechtschild, the eldest of ten, grew up in the mainly Jewish town of Mogielnicza, Poland, the child of a strict, religious father who had high expectations of him. Rebelling against the oppressive Yeshiva school and wanting a more worldly life, he hitched a ride with a non-Jew on the back of his horse and cart to Warsaw to make his fame and fortune. He was ten years old at the time. For the next four years he made his living as a baker's apprentice, sleeping on top of the stoves at night. In his early eighties he still remembered how he narrowly escaped dying of typhoid in a hospital ward packed full of small boys, only two of whom survived out of dozens. This notion of survival was one that both drove him and haunted him like so many of the Asekaiyi Jews that narrowly escaped the Holocaust.

Josef saved enough money to buy a passage to the promised land, Palestine: a land where one could live as a free man away from the constraints of entrenched anti-Semitism. This notion, which must have seemed to him a distant dream, is a concept that many of my generation and of my background have little to no understanding. (It is only recently after visiting Poland myself and witnessing the near-elimination of a subculture that I am able to understand the immense passion that many Jews of his era must have felt about the settlement of a free Jewish 'homeland'.)

At this point in the narrative Josef pulls out an old faded photograph of a handsome young man in a trilby and overcoat standing beside his parents and siblings. His parents are wearing traditional black orthodox clothes, his father's beard is long and his mother's face gaunt with hardship. He already looks urbane and out of place. Although the face in the photo is that of a man, both in his bearing and behind the eyes, Josef is a mere fourteen years old. Like many of his generation, he never experienced the luxury of childhood or adolescence. It is a photo of the last time he ever saw his parents, on a visit back to the *shtetl* just before he left on the ship bound for Palestine. He never saw his parents again.

In Palestine Josef worked as a confectioner and pastry cook, saving enough money to import a beautiful cousin of his from Poland that he wanted to marry. However, she abandoned him after her arrival—he always claimed that she ended up married in America with a neo-Nazi as a son, wishful thinking I suspect. Now lonely and working furiously, he was matchmade with my grandmother Esther, who herself was recovering from a broken heart.

Tel Aviv in the late 1920s was a young dusty city full of displaced refugees searching for surrogate family. The myth of my grandparents' relationship begins with Josef's story of his wedding night, when he was so inhibited by the presence of his mother-in-law asleep on the couch outside the bedroom that it took him a full three days to complete his nuptial duty.

Josef's Achilles heel was his romanticism regarding women. He had three wives in total: his cousin; Esther, my grandmother, a woman he claims to have been married to for only three weeks; and his last wife, Rachel, to whom he was married in a complex and fairly tortured union for thirty years.

Esther lived in Melbourne, while Josef lived with Rachel in Bondi. The animosity between my grandparents was legendary; it was the kind of love–hate relationship that can eclipse a whole life. He was always chasing her around the table at family celebrations. After his third wife's death, Josef tried to get back with Esther but she was more comfortable in friendly animosity than domestic intimacy.

Josef always wanted me to marry a Jewish man. Once when I was dating a half-Indian guy I decided that I might try and pass him off as Serphadic. When I tried this cautiously out on Josef he curtly warned me that Serphadic men beat their wives! At that point I gave up trying to please him.

My grandfather remembered Cossacks, the Yeshiva and the assassination of Archduke Ferdinand, which triggered the First World War. He was the last of our family to bridge the gap between a Jewish Poland that no longer existed and a secular sun-blasted country on the edge of a new world.

Josef bought his grave a good fifteen years before he died, and was intensely proud of it. He personally overlooked the design, dictated the detailing, fussed about the location. His one claim to fame was the fact that he was a Cohen, one of the sacred tribe. His greatest regret was the fact that he had no son, just three daughters, so the line would stop with his passing.

The mysterious rituals of the Cohen family always fascinated me, and I could never work out the exact perimeters. Grandpa could not go near the dead and at Jewish funerals would have to sit behind a glass window or stand away from the grave. The irony was that the Rabbi that performed at Josef's funeral was a Cohen, too, so my grandfather's draped and solitary coffin stood outside the chapel while the Rabbi performed the sermon inside. To me it was a poignant sight; the exile exiled. I took comfort in the fact that I knew that Josef would be deeply honoured to have a Cohen perform the final ceremony.

It was a most beautiful funeral, and afterwards, in my aunt's house watching my mother and her twin sisters sitting on low stools, heads covered while the minion of twelve men sang prayers, I had a flash of Josef walking through the many guests, shaking hands, thrilled to have so many honour his life; 'Essen, essen, is the strudel good?'

I was reminded of the stoic atheism of Grandfather Bill, of how without ritual and faith there is nothing to commemorate, to immortalise the passing of a life—only DNA and a family album.

Things Could Be Worse

Lily Brett

Lily Brett was born in Germany and came to Melbourne with her parents in 1948. Her first book, The Auschwitz Poems, *won the 1987 Victoria Premier's Award for poetry, and both her fiction and poetry have won other major prizes, including the 1995 NSW Premier's Award for fiction for* Just Like That. *Lily Brett is married to the Australian painter David Rankin. They have three children and currently live in New York.*

LOLA BENSKY SAW HERSELF on the screen. There she was. She was the second guest on the right at Tsaytl and Motl's wedding in *Fiddler On The Roof*. It was her. The same hair, the same eyes, the same mouth, the same expression.

Now, the Lola on the screen was dancing. Look at her. Her skirts were whirling. She was turning this way and that way. Stepping to the right. Stepping to the left. Now she was clapping and dancing. She was dancing the *hora*. She was dancing the *mitzvah-tensl*. Now Lola Bensky could see that it wasn't her up on the screen in *Fiddler On The Roof*. Lola Bensky couldn't dance.

Lola had tried to dance. At sixteen, when her friends were jiving to Chubby Checker, Bobby Darren and Crash Craddock, Lola had tried to look like a carefree rock'n' roller. She had had the right rope petticoats, the right T-bar shoes, the right lipstick and the right hairstyle. But she had had the wrong expression. She looked anguished, embarrassed and uncomfortable. She had tried to keep smiling through 'Only The Lonely' and 'Boom Boom Baby', but her discomfort had dislodged her smile.

Lola had tried again in her early twenties, when dancing had become more creative. You could make up the movements or follow the go-go dancers. At Ziggy's discotheque, Lola had kept her eyes glued to the go-go dancers. Six go-go dancers danced in cages, suspended from the ceiling. Lola often felt dizzy looking up at the dancers while she copied their arm and leg movements, but Lola had no talent for choreography. Her imagination didn't extend to dance steps. If she couldn't see the go-go dancers, she couldn't dance.

At twenty-three, Lola gave up dancing. She didn't dance again until she met Garth. Garth was a fabulous dancer. Lola clung to Garth as he turned and stepped and twisted around the dance floor. Garth held Lola close to him, and clutched her tightly. From this secure position, Lola Bensky could smile while she danced.

*

Lola had seen herself on the screen before. She had seen herself in old footage of the prisoners of Dachau being liberated by the American army. She knew that the young girl behind the barbed wire fence in Dachau, in front of the ditch filled with dead bodies, was her.

Lola saw herself in photographs, too. She saw herself in photographs of street urchins in the Lodz ghetto. She saw herself in a photograph of a small girl sitting next to her dead mother in the ghetto. She saw herself in photographs of Jewish women smiling for the camera in displaced persons camps.

Lola also looked for relatives in these photographs. She searched through photographs, books and films for members of her family. She looked for the son that her parents had had before the war. She looked for her grandparents. She looked for her aunties and uncles and cousins.

In her handbag she kept a notebook with the names of her parents' parents and brothers and sisters. In this notebook, she also kept an index of the titles of the books on the Holocaust that she owned.

Lola hated the word Holocaust. It was too neatly wrapped into a parcel. There were no loose ends and no frayed edges. The Holocaust. It was nice, compact abstraction. But what else could she say? The alternatives were so wordy. She could say the Nazi extermination of European Jewry. She could say the destruction of the Jews by the Nazis. She could say Hitler's murder of six million Jews.

Lola had a library of over one thousand books on the Holocaust. She had read most of them. Lola had a good memory. She had always had a good memory. She could remember hundreds, if not thousands, of phone numbers. Conversations she had ten years ago, she could recall verbatim. Yet the facts and statistics of the Holocaust flew out of her head. She had to check and recheck the information. Was it in Bergen-Belsen that British troops had found over ten thousand unburied bodies? Was it there in Bergen-Belsen that five hundred inmates a day had died from typhoid and starvation in the week after liberation? Was it in Mathausen that the Nazis had murdered thirty thousand Jews in the last four months of the war? Lola had to check and recheck.

When she was thirty, Lola had begun to ask her parents about their experiences in the war. They had answered her questions, hesitantly at first, but they had answered. Lola had listened. She had listened quietly. She had taken notes. She had tape-recorded some of the conversations. She had videotaped a long interview with each of her parents. And still their stories blurred and wandered in her head.

Lola had been shocked to find that other Jews her age didn't know or couldn't remember what had happened to their parents during the war. Solomon Seitz, with his Oxford D.Phil, didn't know. Susan Shuster, a researcher for the prime minister, couldn't remember. Boris Kronhill, the physicist, had a vague idea. He told Lola that his mother had been in hiding in a convent and his father had been in a labour camp in Russia. Lola knew that Boris had it all wrong. Renia knew the Kronhills and had told Lola that Mrs Kronhill had been in Auschwitz and Mr Kronhill had been hidden in a haystack on a farm in Poland for two years.

Renia and Josl's friends thought that Lola, with all her questions and all her books, was crazy. 'What does she want to read books about concentration camps for?' said Genia Pekelman. 'Does she want to go crazy?'

*

Lola came out of the Adelphi theatre in Mordialloc. Mordialloc was a long way from Russia and the world of Tevya and Tsaytl and Motl.

Lola's mother had died nine months ago. Last night, Lola had been feeling out of kilter. She had seen in the *Herald* that *Fiddler On The Roof* was playing at the Adelphi, and she had decided that she needed to see it. This morning Lola had bought a packet of Fantales and a packet of Minties, and driven for an hour to Mordialloc to catch the early matinée session at the Adelphi.

There had been only five other people in the cavernous

theatre. Lola thought that she and the four elderly women and one very old man must have been the only people in Melbourne who hadn't yet seen *Fiddler On The Roof*.

Now, outside the theatre, Lola felt a bit disconcerted. It was a bright, blue, hot day. Mordialloc looked prosperous. People were eating Chiko rolls and pies in the pizza shop next door to the Adelphi. Poor Tevya had been so poor that he had to carry his milk deliveries himself when his horse had become too old. Here everyone had a car and could afford a milkshake.

Lola bought a custard tart and drove back to Melbourne. On her way home she stopped at Texoform, the factory in which her father worked. Josl had been with Texoform for nine years. Josl's clothing company, Joren Fashions, like many small businesses, had closed down in the seventies. At first Josl had felt devastated. Now, he enjoyed his job at Texoform. He had his own office, and he was in charge of ordering the fabrics. Josl felt as though Texoform was his own company. He was overjoyed when he saved the firm money, and he worked hard to create a high morale and a sense of loyalty among the workers.

Josl was surprised to see his daughter, but then nothing that Lola did really surprised Josl. For many years, Lola had been at odds with herself. At odds with him. At odds with his beloved Renia, who had died just when everything was looking promising. Renia had died when both of her daughters were happily married and her grandchildren were turning out to be everything she had hoped for in her own children.

Josl wiped away the tears that came when he thought about Renia. He still got up early every morning and tiptoed around the bedroom so that he wouldn't disturb her. And every morning he was jolted out of his quiet by the realisation that Renia was no longer there. His darling Renia, the woman he had loved since he was twenty-two and she was sixteen, was dead.

Josl kissed Lola hello. He looked at her. Lola had changed. In her thirties Lola had changed, and all the things that Josl had loved in her as a small child had returned. He had loved her curiosity and her enthusiasm. And he had loved her laugh. When Lola was little she used to laugh and laugh. If something struck her as funny she would laugh with her whole body, with her whole being. She would be completely immersed in her laughter. It used to give Josl so much joy.

'Hi, Dad,' said Lola. 'The photo of Mum looks good on the wall. I like this new office. How are you, Dad?'

'I'm all right, Lola. I'm all right,' Josl answered.

'You know what I did today?' said Lola. 'I drove out to Mordialloc and went to the pictures. I haven't been able to work well lately, and I noticed that *Fiddler On The Roof* was playing, so I went and saw it.'

'You haven't seen *Fiddler On The Roof* before?' said Josl.

'No, I'd never seen it,' said Lola.

'You never saw *Fiddler On The Roof*? But everybody did see *Fiddler On The Roof*. What a picture! I loved *Fiddler On The Roof*. Topol was very good in the film, but that Hayes Gordon, who did play Tevya on the stage in Melbourne, he was terrific. He is not a Jew, yet he was one hundred per cent a Jew on the stage. Your Mum and I, we loved him. We saw him twice. I can't believe that until now you didn't see *Fiddler On The Roof*.'

'I'm glad that I went to see it,' said Lola. 'I loved it. Dad, I know it's not Wednesday, but will you have dinner with us tonight? I'm making a beautiful veal and beef *klops* with sauerkraut.'

'I don't want you to start again with the "Can I eat with you" business,' said Josl. 'I told you, I'll come once a week and that's it. *Klops* with sauerkraut? Is it the same way that Mum made it?' Josl asked.

'It's exactly the way that Mum made *klops* and sauerkraut,' said Lola.

'It is a little bit hard to say no to *klops* with sauerkraut. All right, all right, I will come, but don't put me in this position again. I'm not going to be a burden on you or anybody,' said Josl.

'Dad, you know that it makes us happy to see you,' said Lola.

'OK, Lola, OK. I will come but I won't stay long. I want to have an early night. I didn't sleep so well last night. I started thinking, and I couldn't fall asleep. It's no good to think too much. It can get you so mixed up. I started to feel crazy. First I was thinking about Mum. She did everything right. She was slim, she didn't smoke, she did do exercise, and still she died. She was young. Sixty-three is not old today. Then I started to think about the past, and that maybe what happened to Mum in Auschwitz was what did give her the cancer. After a few hours thinking like this you can think you are crazy. It's better not to think too much,' said Josl.

*

'It's better not to think too much' was something Josl had said repeatedly since Lola was small. Lola had stopped thinking altogether when she was sixteen. Until then she had topped all her classes, played the piano well and won prizes for her French and German poetry recitations. At sixteen she failed two of her five final-year high school subjects. The following year she had passed the two subjects that she had failed and failed the three that she had passed. The third time, to everyone's relief, she passed all five subjects.

Lola had drifted through the next ten years. She became a journalist. She became a wife. She became a mother. She seemed like a good journalist, a good wife and a good mother. But Lola was crooked. She was skew-whiff. She was at an odd angle. And no one noticed.

Arrows of anger and shafts of self-pity pitted her thoughts. Fear ruptured her nights. Fantasies and dreams were intertwined with her daily life. She thought she was Renia and Josl. She thought she had been in the ghetto. She thought she had been in Auschwitz too.

Lola had always been plump. But from the age of sixteen, she grew, slowly and steadily, until she was huge. She grew a cocoon around herself. And in this unoccupied territory, this haven, this no-man's land, Lola, a bit breathless and tired, spent her youth.

Lola didn't start thinking again until she was twenty-six and went to see a psychoanalyst about her weight problem.

'What sort of answer is that to a weight problem?' Renia had said when Lola asked her to look after Julian while she went to the analyst. 'Is this a solution to being fat? To go to a psychiatrist? What sort of a solution is that?' said Renia.

'Lola is going to see an analyst about losing weight?' said Ada Small. 'Why doesn't she go to Weight Watchers? Whoever heard of somebody going to see a doctor for mad people, for *meshuganas*, when she just wants to lose some weight? It's crazy.'

'What about a hypnotist?' suggested Genia.

'What about Limmits biscuits, or the egg-and-grape-fruit diet?' said Renia to Lola. 'I have heard some very good reports about that egg-and-grapefruit diet. You can have as many boiled eggs as you like, as long as you eat half a grapefruit first. Lola, what did we do to deserve the shame of a daughter who goes to see a psychiatrist?'

'You think too much and you don't do enough dieting,' Josl had said. 'Anyway,' he had continued, 'I have heard some not very good things about the Herr Professor, this expensive doctor psychiatrist. I heard he got divorced from a very nice woman. I heard that he is the *meshugana*, not the patients that he treats. The worry about this is making your mother sick. Her daughter is going to see a lunatic doctor. She needs this like a hole in the head.'

Lola had decided that it hadn't been a good idea to ask Renia to babysit Julian. She came to an arrangement with her friend Margaret-Anne. Margaret-Anne would look after Julian twice a week while Lola went to her analyst, and Lola would babysit Margaret-Anne's Jonathan while Margaret-Anne was at meditation classes.

Lola had always had close women friends. She spoke to them every day. She had cooked food for their husbands when her friends were in hospital having children. She had scoured the real estate pages of the newspaper and visited properties with them when they were buying houses. Her friends were her substitutes for sisters.

Although she had tried to see little Jonathan as family, his shit stank and she couldn't understand him. After six months Lola had hired a babysitter for Julian.

Lola had tried other ways of creating a large family. She had arranged book clubs, film clubs and card nights. She had tried to organise a communal housing project. Lola had wanted her friends to sell their houses and build new houses on a large block of land that had come up for sale in Melbourne. This land was fifteen minutes from the city, and had a thousand feet of river frontage. Lola had envisaged a beautiful environment where they could all still have their privacy, but they would be able to develop deeper friendships with each other. They would be able to share some of the domestic drudgeries of having young children, and they would also be able to afford luxuries such as a swimming pool and a tennis court.

Lola had cajoled, arranged, organised, pressed and begged her friends. The proposed project had divided the group. The book and film clubs and the card nights came to an end.

Charlie Goldstein, Lola's old school friend, had asked Lola why this large group of friends no longer spoke to each other.

Lola had replied, 'We were split up by my proposal that we become closer.'

This was a liberated era. Charlie Goldstein, still wide-eyed, had told his partner Hyram that, although Lola Bensky didn't look the type, she had told him, and he had heard it with his own ears, that she had tried to organise a wife-swapping commune.

The news had spread through Melbourne. Mrs Goldstein, Charlie's mother, had rung Renia Bensky.

'Renia darling,' she had said, 'I hear you are having a bit of trouble with Lola. Just be strong, Renia. Like my dear departed mother used to say, "Small children small worries, big children big worries."'

'That idiot Mrs Goldstein rang me today,' Renia had said to Josl that evening. 'She rang to let me know that she knows how fat Lola is. "Be strong, Renia," she said. With friends like Mrs Goldstein, who needs enemies?'

'Renia, darling,' said Josl, after he had agreed that Mrs Goldstein was a philistine, a peasant and an idiot, 'Renia darling, I think that Lola is losing a bit of weight. Do you think there is a chance that that lunatic doctor is doing her some good?'

'Who knows what would do Lola good?' said Renia. 'I think I will make her a dish of zucchinis and tomatoes. I got the recipe from Nusia who got it from Mrs Braunstein who is going to Weight Watchers.'

*

Lola was just leaving Josl's office when he called her back. 'Lola, I nearly forgot. I bought some dog food for you. Pal dog food. The brand Mum always bought. It was on special, so I bought two boxes. I'll put them in the boot for you.'

Lola had inherited her mother's dogs. Lola, who had no interest in dogs or cats, was now the owner of Cleo, Benny and Blacky.

Lola was sure that Renia had been the only Jew in Melbourne to own three dogs. Cleo, Benny and Blacky had all been strays. They had attached themselves to Renia, who couldn't bear to see homeless or hungry animals.

Josl put the boxes of dog food in the car. 'Thanks, Dad,' said Lola. 'I'll see you tonight.'

Lola drove towards St Kilda. She felt better. Seeing *Fiddler On The Roof* had cheered her up, and she was happy that Josl was coming for dinner. She wished that her mother wasn't dead. Why did her mother have to die? In the last few years she and her mother had been getting on so well. Lola's throat constricted with choked tears. She hadn't been able to cry for her mother since the funeral.

On St Kilda Road, Lola started to think about how good her life was. She loved Garth, and he loved her. The kids had turned out well. Julian was a medical student.

'My son is two-thirds of a doctor,' Lola boasted. When Renia was in hospital dying, Renia had told every nurse, every intern, every orderly and every specialist that her grandson was a medical student. It had made Lola weep. It had also consoled her. At least she had given Renia a grandson who had given her a lot of pleasure.

Even when he had been a small boy, Julian had been able to make Renia happy. When Renia was with Julian all her anger evaporated and all her anguish vanished. Renia had played with Julian, fed him, walked with him, talked with him. Lola had felt that little Julian had healed and soothed Renia in a way that her own children had never been able to.

When Julian was older, Renia collected his prizes and certificates. The two of them went for long walks along the beach together. Sometimes, on these walks, people had complimented Renia on her handsome son, and she had glowed. 'Julian is as good at maths as I was,' Renia used to say to Lola. Lola had always been hopeless at maths.

*

Lola arrived at Polonsky's kosher butcher shop. Though her parents had never been Orthodox, Lola bought kosher meat. Josl used to laugh at her. 'The kosher meat is twice the price and it doesn't taste any different,' he would say. Lola knew it was irrational, but she felt that the veal and beef were better for having been blessed.

Mrs Kopper was inside Polonsky's.

'Hello, Lola,' she said, 'and how's things? How are you keeping? Are you and your sister still *broygis* with each other? It's a shocking thing that two sisters should not speak to each other. Thank God your poor dear mother, God rest her soul, didn't see this. It is shocking. I saw your father the other day and he told me how upset he was about you two girls. I tell you, Lola, there was a tear in his eyes. I told him, I said to him, "Josl, things could be worse." And it is true. To make your father feel better I reminded him about the old Sholem Aleichem story. You know, the story about the bags of worries. You don't know this story? You didn't hear about it? Well, I will tell you, Lola.

'There was a village where many people had troubles. They came to the rabbi and said "Rabbi, why do I have to have so much trouble? My neighbour doesn't have such troubles. Why was I chosen to have this trouble?" The rabbi heard these complaints many times. One day the rabbi said that everyone who had troubles should put their troubles in a bag, and bring the bag to the marketplace. The people of the village did this. Then the rabbi said that everyone should choose someone else's bag to take home. When the people got home and saw what was in the bag of troubles that they had chosen, they said, "Oh God, please give me my own troubles back. My own troubles were not so bad." The next day everyone returned to the marketplace to get back his own bag of troubles.'

'Excuse me,' said Mrs Singer. 'I know that you are telling this story, Mrs Kopper, but it is important to tell it right. I don't think that Sholem Aleichem said that many people in the village had troubles, just a few people.'

'All right, all right, Mrs Singer,' said Mrs Kopper. 'What does it matter? That is not so important. What is important is what I was trying to tell Lola. And that is that things can always be worse.'

'I can tell you straightaway about two sisters who are worse,' said Mrs Singer. 'My neighbour has got three nieces. The two younger girls hate the older girl. I hear that she is not such a nice person but that is another story. My neighbour's brother, the girls' father, died last month. The younger girls told their older sister, who lives in Canberra, that the funeral was at eleven o'clock. When the older girl arrived at the cemetery, the funeral was finished, because the funeral was really at ten o'clock. And, of course, everybody was talking about how shocking it was that the older daughter didn't come to her father's funeral.'

Lola knew that things could always be worse. It was something that she had always been sure of. Mr Polonsky gave Lola her minced veal and beef.

'Well, Lola,' he said, 'you are a big star now. A famous person. I see your photograph in the *Jewish News* every week. When you left here last time, Mrs Leber asked me if that was Lola Bensky the writer. "Yes, Mrs Leber," I said. "Lola Bensky always buys her meat and chickens here."'

Lola drove home. At home she prepared the *klops* mixture. This was her mother's recipe. Two eggs, two chopped onions, two grated cloves of garlic, two tablespoons of breadcrumbs, two teaspoons of salt and half a teaspoon of pepper for every kilo of meat. It made a delicious meatloaf.

Lola kneaded and kneaded, listening to the soft sound of the meat on her fingers. The meat and onions and eggs and garlic and breadcrumbs blended into a smooth universe.

Maybe one day she would be able to patch things up with her sister, Lola thought. Although it wasn't really a patching job, more like a total overhaul. She put the *klops* into the oven.

You Cannot Imagine

Arnold Zable

Arnold Zable is an author and storyteller. Formerly a lecturer in the Arts Faculty at Melbourne University, he has worked in the USA, Papua New Guinea, China, and various parts of Europe and Asia. His novel Jewels and Ashes *was published in Melbourne by Scribe in 1991. It won five Australian literary awards, and was published by Harcourt Brace in New York in 1993. Zable is the author of numerous feature articles, short stories, essays, works for Yiddish theatre, and two children's books published by Oxford University Press. His work has appeared in a range of journals and anthologies, and he has been a columnist and feature writer for* The Age. *Zable's most recent book,* Wanderers and Dreamers, *a series of stories based on Yiddish theatre in Australia, was published by Hyland House in 1998.*

'You Cannot Imagine' *is taken from Arnold Zable's novel,* Jewels and Ashes, *published by Scribe in Melbourne, and Harcourt Brace in New York.*

HIS APARTMENT IS ON the second floor of a six-storey tenement; one of several drab grey blocks built up from the ghetto ruins in the immediate post-war years. It is now run down, cracking at the seams, joints wracked by arthritis. The stairs smell of fried onions and neglect. I am ushered into a sparsely furnished living-room with a single bed, table and television set on a linoleum-covered floor.

He is rotund and squat, his substantial paunch offset by muscular shoulders that barely contain an outrageous energy which seems always on the verge of bursting beyond the confines of his tight body. He speaks to me with a conspiratorial air, while his hawk-like eyes, full of an ancient suspicion, dart from side to side, always alert, distracted. Buklinski, one of the very last of the Bialystoker Jews, has burst into my life.

Buklinski disappears into the kitchen and dashes back with plates of stewed potatoes and gefilte fish. 'Imported from Hungary', he announces triumphantly, jabbing his fingers at the fish. He runs back and forth from the kitchen, and soon the table is laden with bowls of herring, pickled onions, loaves of bread, cheeses, and several bottles of vodka. Buklinski seats himself opposite and commands, in a voice strewn with gravel. '*Nu?* Eat! Is anyone stopping you! Who are you waiting for! The Messiah?' He speaks a rich colloquial Yiddish laced with earth, fire and black humour. Looking at me, he muses: 'A miracle! Our Bialystoker have wandered off to the very ends of the earth in all their dark years, and yet their sons speak Yiddish. A miracle! *Nu?* What are you waiting for? Eat!'

The vodka flows. Buklinski's monologue accelerates. He weaves tall stories in a frenzy. 'I was born on Krakowska, in the Chanaykes, in that very same neighbourhood your mother lived in. We were crammed on top of each other; slept three, four, sometimes more to a bed. We froze in winter, baked in summer, and roamed the streets in gangs of little scoundrels who hunted in packs, seeing with our own eyes everything the heart desired— swindlers and saints, devoted mothers and beggars, prostitutes and yeshiva boys scurrying home, their eyes glued to their sacred books as they bumped into lamp posts. Ah, what a treasure it was to live in Bialystok! Well, my friend, what else could we do but love it? You think we had a choice? Well? What are you waiting for? Eat! Drink! Don't be shy!'

Whenever one dish is empty, Buklinski dashes back into the kitchen and emerges with reinforcements, plates piled high with cheese *blintzes*.

'This is my specialty, which you must eat.'

'You are like a Yiddishe mama,' I protest.

'I'm better than a Yiddishe mama. No Yiddishe mama makes *blintzes* like mine.'

'But I'm full. I can hold no more.'

'Full. Shmul. There is always room for more. Eat! I cannot rest until I see you eat.'

Buklinski hovers around the table, restless, imploring, prodding, scolding: 'Eat! I won't sit down until you eat!'

Where have I heard these familiar words, the same pleas, this same script? Where have I seen that same intensity, and felt that same tinge of menace in the voice? I have known other Buklinskis. They stood in Melbourne homes, by tables overflowing with food and drink, and talked of hunger and mud.

'In two things I am an expert,' Zalman would say. Zalman, the family friend, the Bialystoker, the survivor who had brought us tales from the kingdom of night. 'About two things I know all there is to know. In these things I am a scholar, an expert, a professor. In all other things I may be an ignoramus, but on two subjects I can lecture for days on end and never come to the end of it: mud and hunger. We lived in mud. For six years we were soaked in it. We came to know its subtle changes in texture, from day to day, hour to hour, depending on the amount of rain, the number of wagons and dragging feet that churned it up, the number of work battalions that laboured through it. The ghetto was an empire of mud. And hunger. Hunger had so many nuances, so many symptoms. Sometimes you felt so light, so empty, you could fly. But always it was an infernal ache, a relentless yearning, a search for any possible thing that could be chewed and swallowed. And now I know that a kitchen must be full, and a man is a fool who does not seize a chance to eat...'

But this is no time to philosophize. Buklinski has opened a second bottle of vodka. He is up on his feet, dancing around the table like a boxer between rounds. I try to break into his monologue from time to time, but Buk-

linski is a bulldozer who flattens me with his manic, domineering, frenzied, suspicious, yet affectionate energy. One
moment he has his arms around me, and is kissing my
cheeks with joy while exclaiming how good it is to have
such a guest, a son of Bialystoker come half-way around
the planet, the grandson of Bishke Zabludowski, no less,
whom we all knew, and who didn't know him as he stood
under the town clock selling newspapers, telling us what
was going on in this twisted world, and now, can you
believe it, his grandson has come to us from the very
ends of the earth, like manna falling from the heavens. A
miracle!

And the next moment he is wheeling and dealing, and
claiming all foreigners have a dollar to spare and that
money grows on trees over there, while we are stuck here,
in this black hole, our friends old or dead, the clever ones
gone, scattered over lands of milk and honey, while we,
may the devil have such luck, we languish here where there
aren't even enough Jews left for a quorum. So? What
would it hurt to spare us a dollar? What harm would it do
to give us a little something? And just as I think Buklinski
has got me against the ropes he is suddenly off and running again, propelled into the kitchen by a burst of
obsessive generosity to fetch a third bottle of vodka,
another plate of pickled herring. *Nu?* What are you waiting for? Drink! Eat!

The room is bursting with heat and words. Buklinski
jerks off his jacket. I see tattoos on both arms: a mermaid
curls around one forearm, and on the other a muddy-blue
clumsily applied number sprawls through a scattering of
grey hair. 'Two years,' he says quietly when he catches me

looking. 'For two years I was in Auschwitz.' All words grind to an abrupt halt. Buklinski sits at the table, his head propped up on his elbows, his gaze extending beyond me, far beyond the confines of the apartment. Tears, just one or two, replace his torrent of words. They travel crookedly along paths that weave across a face engraved with furrows and troughs, the face of a member of an almost extinct tribe, one of the last Jews of Bialystok.

*

Buklinski is running ahead, dragging me by the arm. 'No one knows Bialystok as well as I do,' he repeats for at least the fifth time this morning. In motion Buklinski is a tubby dynamo, fuelled by nervous energy and raw suspicion, trotting on his stout little legs. His stomach, the receptacle for a thousand-and-one meals of gefilte fish washed down by vodka, protrudes and bounces as he drives himself along. Head held high, hooded eyes squinting in the sun, nose sniffing the air, Buklinski nears the streets of the Chanaykes.

'This is my territory, Ulitza Krakowska. Here I was born. In 1919.' His words tumble out, breathless, between gulps of air. His fingers stab at the empty space where his house once stood. The Chanaykes is an amalgam of weed-strewn clearings, cobblestoned streets, and rheumatic timber cottages. We are on home turf, and Buklinski is a weather vane registering every slight shift in the atmosphere. His arms swing in one direction, then in another, a stream of anecdotes flowing from his fingers. 'That was a bordello,' he exclaims. 'The boss lived upstairs, there, in the garret. I often saw his face poking out of that window, eyeing the customers who used to sneak in through that wooden gate. Fifty groshen it cost for doing it standing up, and one whole zloty for doing it lying down.'

Buklinski is unable to keep still. It is as if the streets are pursuing him and that, if he were to stop for long enough, they could lure him into a web of memories that would soon suffocate him. So he keeps running ahead, with short steps, while conducting a feverish commentary: 'This was once a prayer-house; that building housed a kibbutz where young pioneers prepared for the Promised Land. Over there stood a Hebrew college; here a Yiddish trade school.' Occasionally I register a deeper response, jolted by a sudden shock of recognition. The trade school features in my mother's repertoire of recollections; in this school she had learned to make dresses. 'Ah! You see? I know where to take you,' Buklinski proclaims triumphantly. 'I know my Bialystok.'

On Ulitza Slonimska flocks of pigeons swoop down to perch on the window-sills of pre-war buildings. Their grey facades are a patchwork of exposed brick blotches coated with rust. We veer sharply into a narrow alley, to a timber shop-front painted clumsily in a pale blue wash. It leans askew, like a dilapidated shed on an abandoned farm. Inside the workshop Yankel the shoe repairer stands bent over a bench, cutting strips of leather. I am also introduced to Bunim, who is seated by the counter, his shoulders slumped, his head swaying as if in perpetual prayer.

'Bunim! Get us a bottle of schnapps!' Buklinski orders. 'Here! Take these zlotys and fetch us something to drink, something to bite.' Half an hour later the compliant Bunim shuffles back with a bottle of spirits. We tear chunks from a loaf of freshly baked bread, slice pieces of garlic and sausage, drink glass after glass of spirits, and the room blazes.

'Aron! Welcome to Bialystok!' Yankel exclaims after each toast. The room spins about us, a blur of shelves piled high with shoes, pieces of leather, soles and heels, tacks and nails, and workbenches crowded with an array of primitive tools with which to cut and glue, hammer and sew, brush and polish, while Yankel is drinking, working, and proclaiming: 'Aron! You cannot imagine what it was like!' This is the refrain to which he constantly returns, as his story unfolds in a workshop saturated with the smell of garlic and sweat. 'You cannot imagine! We were hunted like animals, swatted like flies. Wives in front of husbands. Children in front of mothers. Aron! You cannot imagine what it was like!'

Yankel's eyes are sunk deep in their sockets, and nestle behind cheekbones that protrude, stretching taut the layer of beaten skin that clings to its skeletal frame. 'We ran like frightened hares into the countryside and burrowed under the ground. For two years I hid in my warren. At night I emerged to scavenge. Lice made a home in my flesh. We had a contract: I lived in a hole; they lived on me. Aron! You cannot imagine what it was like!'

This is what it is always like, I am beginning to see, when the last few Yidn of Bialystok gather, as they often do, since they crave each other's company; together they wax and wane like candles that flicker for a moment into glorious light, and then almost die out, as the flames shrink back into themselves, into indelible memories that will

Enough Already

accompany them to the grave. 'When I came out of my warren for the final time, on a July day in 1944, I saw four Russian soldiers on horseback. The lice were crawling around me, going on family visits. I addressed the captain in Yiddish. He looked at me in astonishment and replied in the same mother tongue: "A living corpse! A survivor! A miracle!" He escorted me to the nearest village where he organised a banquet. I ate until I was sick.'

Several hours later I walk with Bunim, Bialystok's most dishevelled son. He shuffles, chin sunk into his chest. Occasionally he glances warily over his shoulders. 'Someone is always watching, always taking note,' he warns. The Sabbath is approaching, creeping in along deserted streets that have retired for the weekend. The sky is streaked with wafer-thin clouds of mauve and crimson; Bunim is, as usual, close to tears. This is what Buklinski had warned me about: 'Watch out for him. Just give him a chance and he'll cry. Ah! Can he cry!' He was the butt of many jokes that winked between Yankel and Buklinski. 'Look! It's coming! The storm is gathering. Bunim is about to cry. Ah! Can he cry!'

'Don't make such a noise,' a perpetually anxious Bunim had said when our revelry had begun to shake the floorboards of Yankel's workshop. 'It's not wise for us to attract attention. You must always remember who we are and who they are,' he had added, while motioning towards the window. 'Bunim is going to cry. It's coming! Ah! Can he cry!' replied the merciless duo, dancing arm-in-arm around the work benches.

Bunim's apartment is lean and bare, and mother Mary peers down at us, a babe with golden locks in her arms.

228

The last shafts of light from a dying day poke into the kitchen, illuminating layers of peeling paint and cracks that thread through the walls like erratic blood vessels.

Bunim slumps into a chair and leans back against the wall. 'Bialystok is a stranger to me now, the streets are my enemies. I have wanted to leave for many years. One by one my friends have gone. But I must stay because she saved my life. For three years she hid me, fed me, and gave me warmth. So after the war I married her. She prays to an alien God. Christ is her saviour. And I'm not even worth his piss. You see my friend, she saved my life and I must stay with her.'

When Bunim speaks, the words are barely audible. He is almost a non presence, mumbling in the background, as if afraid to register his imprint upon the earth. The permanent red blotches on his cheeks deepen to beetroot in the evening shadows. The silence within the apartment seems to offer solace and relief, and for the first time there is a hint of ease on Bunim's unshaven face. 'I knew your grandfather,' he says unexpectedly. 'Everyone knew your grandfather. A small man. With red hair, a red beard, he ran here and there under the clock-tower, always excited, always darting about like a rabbit. *Heint! Moment! Express!* Always shouting, selling, waving his arms, earning a few groshen from his newspapers. *Heint! Moment! Express!*'

Bunim rises from the chair, a sudden flicker of animation in his leaden body, his bloodshot eyes aflame, the words tumbling out rapid fire, his voice reaching above whispers: '*Heint! Moment! Express!* He stood on the corner of Geldowa and Kupietzka, just a block from here. Everyone knew your grandfather. *Heint! Moment! Express!*'

And, just as abruptly as it has risen, Bunim's voice trails off into a confused monologue, and his body slumps back into a chair: 'My father wanted me to be a talmudic scholar. I studied in yeshivas with great interpreters of the scriptures. But she saved my life, and I'm not even worth her piss. Children we could not have. That would have been a terrible transgression, an insult to my ancestors. And Bialystok I could not leave. That would have been a betrayal. After all, she saved my life...'

Everyone has his story; everyone his refrain. Aron! You cannot imagine what it was like! Aron! Do you know what a treasure it was to live in Bialystok? Aron! She saved my life and I'm not worth her piss. Aron! Eat. Drink. What are you waiting for? The Messiah? Aron! Do you know how wonderful it was to live in Bialystok? Aron! Please stay with us a little longer. Aron! Help us leave this God-forsaken hole. Take us with you to the land of milk and honey. Aron! I cannot leave. She saved my life. Aron! Spare us a dollar. What would it hurt to give? Aron! Eat! Drink! What are you waiting for? The Messiah? Aron! You can never imagine what it was like.

Paris

Ron Elisha

Ron Elisha was born in Jerusalem in 1951 and migrated with his family to Melbourne in 1953.

His stage plays include In Duty Bound, Einstein, Two, Pax Americana, The Levine Comedy, Safe House, Esterhaz, Impropriety *and* Choice. *He has also written a telemovie,* Death Duties, *two children's books,* Pigtales *and* Too Big, *and many feature articles in a variety of publications.*

His plays have been produced throughout Australia, New Zealand, United States, United Kingdom, Canada and France, and have won a number of awards, including four Australian Writers' Guild Awards and an International Film Festival Award.

His recent work includes projects for stage, screen and multimedia.

He works as a general practitioner, is married and has two children.

Excerpt 1

Rabbi Mendel Brot finds himself in Paris, on an enforced sabbatical. Alone, and highly myopic, he very soon loses not only his way but, also, the ancient Torah *scroll he has brought with him by way of a gift. His search for the scroll implicates him in a fatal car accident, as a result of which he is taken into police custody. It is here that he has cause to reflect.*

Excerpt 2

A fugitive on the lam, Rabbi Mendel Brot stands atop the Arc de Tiomphe, from which vantage point his accessory in crime, a French toilet cleaner by the name of Henri Bergson, affords him a rare perspective.

AS FAR AS MENDEL could tell, it had all begun six months earlier, in the midst of a eulogy he was delivering at the graveside of Zachariah Nussbaum, a twelve-year-old boy who had died suddenly as the result of a freak lightning strike.

The scene, of course, was an horrific one. The boy's mother, unable to support herself, wept and screamed till Mendel thought that his own heart would leap from his mouth with the pain of her grief. The boy's father, his eyelids red and swollen to the point of closure, stood with his back to her, surrounded by friends and relatives, yet oblivious of all. He seemed numb, his supply of tears completely exhausted, and simply stared at the fresh, cold earth that now covered what, nineteen hours earlier, had been the warm, animated joy of his life.

Almost the entire congregation surrounded the graveside, weeping, aching, trying to imagine their own pain if such a tragedy were ever to befall their own children, as if by so doing they could lessen the possibility of the unthinkable actually occurring.

Mendel himself always found the eulogy of a child extraordinarily difficult. There was no life to recount—the child had barely lived. No momentous acts of charity, no great and lasting legacy, no wisdom, no particular humour that might mark off the child from the great mass of the world's youthful dead, nothing that might ordinarily be seen as the fruit of a long life, fully lived. In spite of this, or perhaps because of it, there was a desperate need amongst those who remained to imbue the death of one so young with some greater, subtler meaning.

On this particular day, more than any other, the urgency of that quest was more deeply felt than ever. This murderous bolt of lightning—more than any other cataclysmic event—was most surely an act of God. Why? Why lightning? Why then? Why in that particular spot? Would the world have been any worse off had the bolt struck a mere twenty metres to one side? Why would it suit God's purpose to murder an innocent boy a mere week before his

Bar Mitzvah? The pressure on Mendel to provide a satis-
factory answer was enormous.

And he could remember the moment—the very
moment—when he first felt the urge. It was in the midst
of the sentence: '...It could be said that a boy who dies at
the age of twelve has lived a perfect life...'. On the word
'perfect'. That was when he felt it rise beneath his
diaphragm. A sudden, subtle thrust, causing a tiny rush of
air to be expelled from his nostrils. At first, he thought
nothing of it. A particle of dust, perhaps, inhaled in the
process of drawing breath in order to be heard over the
sound of communal mourning.

But there was no cough. Only a vague tightening of
the muscles at the angles of the jaw, together with those at
the corners of the mouth. And then, suddenly, another
blast of air, rushing from his nostrils.

The muscles at the corners of his mouth twitched,
then quivered. Was he about to weep? He passed the back
of a knuckle over his eye. There were no tears. Once more,
he felt his diaphragm convulse, followed by a rapid sucking in of air. Was he about to faint? The sensation was the
oddest he had ever experienced in his life. Another con-
vulsion, and...

Laughter. Not a mere giggle, nor a guffaw, nor even
the kind of hysterical laughter one often associates with
moments of great trauma. No. This was a full-bodied, full-
throated belly-laugh, rising—or so it seemed—from the
very marrow of his consciousness. And it was not a single
volley, but a cascade that built upon itself, making it impossible for him to continue the eulogy.

At first, the mourners around him took the sounds that

now emanated from the good *rebbe* to be those of anguished weeping. Such an interpretation notwithstanding, most were either shocked or shaken by the sight of the great man—a man who, over a lifetime of service to the community, had surely seen the very best and the very worst that life had to offer—so completely overwhelmed by the passion of his grief.

But then, as the holy man staggered back, unable to continue, holding his belly lest it burst with the ferocity of his mirth, an alarming note of doubt entered their minds. Had the man of God, transfigured by grief, actually lost his mind?

Mendel himself was in no condition to enlighten them. Incapacitated by the physical effort of laughter, he struggled to comprehend the emotions that had led to its sudden and shameful eruption. What, in the name of God, standing in the centre of a grief-stricken community, at the feet of a dead boy, had he found amusing?

To his eternal shame, Mendel had to be escorted away from the graveside, not even only so far as the chapel, but all the way to the street outside the front gate to the cemetery, where the ringing peals of his preposterous hilarity could no longer offend those within.

That very evening, immediately after the *minion* at the home of the deceased's family (a *minion* at which, incidentally, Mendel had not been permitted to officiate), an emergency board meeting was held in the inner sanctum of the synagogue's administrative chambers.

At one end of the long, polished table sat Mendel, as imposing as ever, attired in black coat and *shtroymel*.

Gathered at the other end of the table, as if for fear of contracting some vile, subversive germ that might undermine the sanctity of the holy place in which they sat, were four members of the synagogue's board: Shmuel Perlman, Godel Moshinsky, Lev Marcovicz and the cantor, Yehuda Freiheit.

'Nu, *Rebbe*,' said Yehuda, making it obvious that an explanation of the day's events was in order. Mendel noted, with more than a little sadness, that his friend of almost 50 years had chosen to jettison the usual 'Mendel' in favour of the more formal '*Rebbe*'.

There was a long, thought-filled pause.

'What can I say?' shrugged Mendel. 'I laughed.'

Another pause.

'Even Sarah herself laughed, in the very face of God, when He informed her, in all seriousness that, at the age of ninety years, she would still bear a child.'

'That wasn't in the midst of *death*,' barked Godel, never easily impressed.

'No—it was at the very prospect of *life*,' responded Mendel, almost daring to smile.

'Is that the best you can do?' asked Lev, biting at a too-bitten cuticle. He was already thinking of what they could possibly tell an angry and bewildered congregation.

'It just happened,' said Mendel, slamming his palm down upon the table by way of emphasis. 'Bang. Just like that. An act of God.'

'You're saying God made you laugh,' Shmuel seemed honestly to be searching for an answer that would have some meaning.

'Why not?' Mendel rose to his full height, and moved away from the table. 'If He can cause lightning to strike down a twelve-year-old boy, isn't it possible that He might also cause laughter to strike at the boy's funeral? Which of the two, I ask, is the more shameful act?'

The members of the board were almost as stunned as they had been at the cemetery earlier that day. They looked at one another, unsure as to how to proceed. Before them, larger than life, stood a man they had known and revered for the better part of a lifetime. A deeply devout man, of wisdom and of principle. And now, for the first time, an ecclesiastical time-bomb.

'We're concerned,' ventured Shmuel, 'that this…aberration might occur again.'

'Laughter?' Mendel raised his thick eyebrows. 'An aberration?'

'*Inappropriate* laughter.' Godel left a hefty beat between the two words.

'What do you want?' Mendel leaned forward, supporting himself on the table. 'A written guarantee?'

'Do you have any idea how the boy's parents are going to feel?' asked Lev. 'In the months and years to come. When they begin to emerge from the fog. And begin to recall what actually happened on this day. Begin to recall that it was the death of their son—their only son—which brought the great *Rebbe*, Mendel Brot—for the first time in almost fifty years of service—to his knees with uncontrolled mirth. Do you have any idea what they're going to feel as they carry that thought throughout the remainder of their pitiful lives?'

'Anger,' whispered Mendel, so softly that, at first, the word escaped almost unnoticed. 'It was anger.'

'Anger!? Anger's not even a tenth of it!' Godel's face grew exceedingly red.

'No no—that's what *I* felt. Anger.'

'You!?'

'Yes.'

'What do you mean, "you"!?'

'I felt anger.'

'And that made you *laugh*?'

Mendel nodded.

'Forgive me for saying so, *Rebbe*,' said Godel, 'but that's not normal. For a man—and *what* a man—to laugh—and *what* a laugh—in the midst of a solemn—and *what* a solemn—occasion, and to attribute that laughter to an emotion—and *what* an emotion—other than mirth. I'm sorry, but that's not normal.'

'You're probably right,' Mendel agreed. 'But are we put on this Earth merely to be normal?'

'Most of us must be, or the word wouldn't exist.' Yehuda began to chuckle at his own conceit, felt the alarmed gaze of his colleagues upon him, and realised that he too was now under suspicion of having fallen prey to the demonic influence that had inhabited the cemetery that afternoon.

'What, precisely, did you feel anger *about*?' asked Shmuel, measuring his words carefully.

'I've been thinking about that. All afternoon.' Mendel shrugged. 'I'm really not sure. Whether it was anger with the Almighty, for having allowed such a thing. Or at the congregation, for demanding that I imbue such a senseless tragedy with meaning. Or at myself...'

'For what?' Shmuel leaned closer.

'Doubt?'

A collective (though silent) sigh filled the room. The board knew it had a problem on its hands.

'Perhaps you should consider a change,' said Lev, ever careful to avoid the use of the word 'holiday', which had been known to elicit in the good *Rebbe* a reaction even more violent than that occasioned by doubt.

'So you see,' said Mendel to his enthralled listener, 'I've been sent to Paris to regain my faith.'

*

Mendel considered his options.

'What if I get rid of these clothes?'

'With a beard like yours, they could spot you for a rabbi from the other end of the *Champs Elysees*.'

Mendel's gaze turned to the proud avenue. At its far end, past the now ghostly silhouette of the *Obelisque*, was the outline, pale in the mist, of what looked like another triumphal arch. He applied his second lens, and was able to make out the silhouettes of the rear ends of a group of thundering stallions atop the arch. In place of this apocalyptic image, he tried to imagine the spectre of a lone rabbi, spectacles glinting in the sun, beard streaming in the wind, perched perilously at the mouth of the awesome *Louvre*.

'We have to find a way of getting you out of the country.'

'Back home?' Mendel couldn't remember the last time he had thought of home. What sort of home was it, he pondered, that deserted a man's consciousness in his hour of greatest need. A sudden pang of emptiness struck at the place where he imagined his heart to be.

It was true, certainly, that the good *rebbe* had been married. On more than one occasion.

As was the tradition amongst orthodox Jewish families at the time, the first marriage had been an arranged one. The girl, Ruchel Jabotinsky, two years his junior at sixteen years of age, was a good girl from a good family. The couple met for the first time at the altar, and their eyes first met only after vows had already been exchanged and Ruchel's veil had been drawn aside.

From the moment her face became visible, Mendel's heart sank. Not because she was physically unattractive— Mendel recognised that his own, heavily bespectacled appearance left much to be desired—but because her eyes betrayed a flatness that negated the existence of a soul in anything but the strictly religious sense. The good *rebbe* felt like his forefather, Jacob who, upon unveiling Leah, realised that he would have to work for Lavan for another seven years in order to earn the hand of her sister. Only for Mendel, there were no second chances.

They kissed. Her lips were moist. Too moist. Their hands were joined. Hers were plump and damp with perspiration.

From that moment, Mendel knew that he would never find anything in the marriage beyond a kind of bored irritation. What made it worse, in a way, was the sense that she felt exactly the same way about him. They had failed each other from the very outset. The marriage was doomed.

The wedding night was an awkward affair. Each party knew what was expected, but neither approached the task with anything remotely approaching relish. Ruchel's body was quite comely, and she did her best to perform whatever manoeuvres she believed might best bring the good *rebbe* to climax. But it was useless. The marriage was not consummated. On that night or any other.

Every morning thereafter, Mendel, upon finishing his morning prayers, added a fervent plea that the Almighty might grant him the strength of resolve to see out the marriage.

The good Lord promptly answered his prayers. He did so by striking down Ruchel with a highly anaplastic malignant melanoma of the left eye, which had to be enucleated, leaving an enormous cavern where the left side of her face had been. The cancer itself, however, had already spread throughout her comely body and, within the space of six months, had killed her. Mendel's resolve, therefore, easily passed the test.

His second wife, Mindla Bluzjstein, presented a greater challenge. Blessed with eyes that could stop traffic, she brought to the marriage a degree of independent reason that Mendel found difficult to assimilate into his view of the traditional conjugal state. Not twenty minutes into the wedding night, this independence of reason was brought to bear in the matter of contraception.

For his own part, Mendel saw no reason to use any. Mindla, on the other hand, produced a half-used packet of the Pill. Her objections—and hormonal status—notwithstanding, a child was sired upon her that very night. Having offered up his thanks for this miraculous chromosomal serendipity, Mendel prayed that the child would lead a happy life, never knowing the meaning of the word 'suffering'.

Once again, his obliging Creator answered his prayers.

The child—a boy, name of Solomon Eliezer Brot—was born, drew precisely seven breaths and died.

Whilst it was technically true that Solomon Eliezer had never known the meaning of the word 'suffering', the good *rebbe* could not help feeling more than a little cheated. His bountifully eyed wife, however, bypassed a sense of mere injustice in favour of moral outrage. Within four hours of the death, she had jettisoned all faith—within six, her husband to boot. The good *rebbe*, she made it plain, was merely the earthly drone of Divine Evil.

The last Mendel had heard, some years later, Mindla was working in a circus, on the receiving end of a series of very sharp knives. Appalled yet curious, the good *rebbe* himself had made it his business to witness a performance, and winced at the shuddering impact of each knife as it struck its mark, just millimetres from the still supple flesh that framed the then fading eyes that had once quickened his pulse. Mindla, on the other hand, didn't turn so much as a greying hair. That she had by then chosen to place her faith in *some*thing was abundantly clear. What that something was, precisely, remained a mystery to the man of God, who left by a side entrance when the elephants were brought on.

Mendel's third wife, Esther Novytager, had been the apple of his increasingly myopic eye. Combining all the virtues most highly prized in a wife of a man of the cloth— not least amongst which was the ability to spot, deflect and disarm the overzealous congregant—she had been attracted to the good *rebbe* by the sense that hidden somewhere behind that expansive beard lay an often deeply buried sense of irony bordering on the blasphemous.

This third and final marriage brought to Mendel Brot the kind of joy which, hitherto, he had believed to be the exclusive province either of the virtuous deceased or, alternatively, the ridiculously wealthy, for whom happiness was merely another commodity. Every morning, therefore, at the end of his prayers, he offered up thanks to his great Benefactor, entreating Him to grant His humble servant many more years of married bliss.

Having complied with the *rebbe*'s previous wishes, the Great and Forgiving One apparently felt under no great obligation to meet the latest in what must have perpetually seemed an endless list of demands. Consequently, after ten years and the birth of four children, the Good Lord saw fit to bring to a close the formidable Esther's sojourn upon the earth by having her forget a jar of pickled cucumbers at the checkout counter, go back to reclaim it and be shot in the abdominal aorta at point-blank range by a crazed gunman who blamed the New World Corporation for modern society's loss of traditional values.

Utterly devastated, the good *rebbe* had resolved never to remarry.

His children, too, had gone their separate ways.

There was Mottel, reputed to have been born with spectacles, who had grown to become a rabbi in his own right, had vied with his father for a chance at the community's helm and, when shunned as spiritually callow by men so worldly that they could no longer recall where they were the day President Kennedy was assassinated, had fled to a community on the African continent where, it was said, he had been ceremoniously eaten by savages. No body parts were ever recovered.

Then came Asher, a small-boned, affectionate child, bright and well-behaved, who brought an abundance of love and joy to the hearts of all those whose lives he touched right up until the day he himself was touched by God, a benediction that resulted in the diagnosis of chronic paranoid schizophrenia. Those whom he had once loved now became the object of vicious and unrestrained opprobium until, by the time he was thirty, he could survive from one birthday to the next without having occasion to use a familiar name. Birthdays themselves were no exception to this rule.

The next was Malka, a lively and robust girl for whom great hopes were held. Generous and friendly almost to a fault, she brought into the Brot household an air of busy excitement that was without precedent. Possessed of a maturity beyond her years, described by her teachers as 'a natural-born mother', precocious in her assumption of the fully developed female form, it seemed only a matter of a handful of years before she would carry the Brot genetic endowment into the next millennium. It was as she was poised on the very edge of this great adventure that she entered into her first lesbian relationship. Despite a long and exhaustive search through the seminal texts of the Judaic tradition, Mendel was never able to find a passage that spoke in encouraging terms of such a liaison. Relations were correspondingly icy.

The last child, Ephraim, uttered his first words at four months, spoke fluently at six, mastered Hebrew at nine, committed the Torah, Talmud and Mishnah to memory by the time he was four years of age and, at the tender age of six years, declared himself an atheist. Despite Mendel's best efforts to the contrary, his wayward son remained firm in his resolve. The chasm of belief grew to a canyon across which, with the passage of the years, each found it progressively more difficult to hear the increasingly distant voice of the other. As far as Mendel could ascertain—adrift, as it were, in the midst of this echoing silence—God still had not revealed himself to Ephraim.

The result of the foregoing circumstances was that, for Mendel, the notion of home held no special attraction. Home was everywhere and nowhere—a bitterly romantic notion in the troubled mind of a reluctantly wandering Jew.

The Violin-maker, the Forest and the Clock

Alex Skovron

Alex Skovron was born in Poland and arrived in Australia in 1958, after spending fifteen months in Israel; his family settled in Sydney, where he lived for more than two decades. Over the past twenty-five years he has worked as a book editor for a number of publishers, and in the late 1970s was general editor of The Concise Encyclopaedia of Australia. *He now lives in Melbourne and works as a freelance editor. Alex Skovron's poetry has been published widely, and three collections have appeared to date:* The Rearrangement *(1988), which won the Anne Elder and Mary Gilmore awards, and was shortlisted in the NSW Premier's Awards;* Sleeve Notes *(1992); and* Infinite City *(1999). He was a recipient of an Australia Council writer's grant for 1994, and has been a winner of the Wesley Michel Wright Prize for Poetry (1983), the John Shaw Neilson Poetry Award (1995, for 'The Violin-maker, the Forest and the Clock'), and the Manuel Gelman Memorial Price for Literature (1997). He has also published several short stories, has completed a novella, and is working towards a fourth book of poems.*

I

Into the thatched night
along the rickety wagon-rutted road
that curved beyond the village
with its fourteenth-century church
and its yard of graves and its cross
and the infinite well creaking
on its thick bucket like a bad G
(or the salty delicious hum of the sea
imagined by ages of children fresh
from fables and antique deceits told night
after night by twinkling old fathers
and aunts), reaching deep
into a difficult earth where water
and blood cleanse a geology
creased by the grating of the earth's teeth
against teeth and teeth against time
and the subterranean wind
washes the rock's knowledge and its dream...

Beyond the chicken-scattered dusk
winding along the forest edge
like a farmyard ghost, into

the line of glittering firs
that escort the road, into the wood
darkening under its cool brood,
the irony of trunks that loom
to define and defend the roof of the day,
where footsteps lose themselves in
swift leaves, where sound tapers down
to the rustle of a faraway sun
somewhere above and beyond the trees,
down to the essence of sound, the beat
of the heart and the humming lilt
of the season's sap running deep
through the earth, the hypnotic trunks
reaching beyond thought, the clustered
guilts of mushrooms, cream and tawny and red,
sucking into the roots' slopes
against the gathering trees...

Past tangled ferns and darked
clearings and slopes flooded with petals
of all imaginable hues, rushing
undulant into the distance of clocks,
swimming drunk among loops
of forgotten streams, berry-provendered
apple and pumpkin and sunflower
resonant earths, and
creaking bridges and stiles a thousand
memories old, like the half-sunken machines
or rusting wheels of abandoned mines
and forgotten rail-ways scrubbed
into the pre-industrial earth, girders

and shafts and indecipherable parts
strewn in the jealous grass like thoughts
too difficult to bury or too strange,
and faint pathways etched only just
within the grasp of sight
uneasy and familiar as a dream
of destinations too dark to name...

    And there it is. Call it a cottage
or a forest house leaning on its hip, thatched
to the hilt, the straw benign but holding up
a roof that would collapse if required
to account for itself, yet a too straight
peruke, like the dowdy concert-goers
at the Imperial Court longing to be crowned
in their dotage by the sprig of youth
but caring when all is said and nothing done
only for the music after all.

    Come closer. The walls must be of wood,
the chimney hints at smoke, the door, buried
amid a husk of ferns and flower-buckets,
ancient barrows and a box of rope, is
overarched with strays of willow-blossom
from the sobbing patrician trunk
that guards the gravelly yard, the sparrows
flecked with dust, and an abandoned wagon
bristling with broken hopes.

    Approach, push through the surprising door.
Enter a world.

II

In front of a bench he stands,
the century scrawled across his features.
The room is hung with shadows:
from every wall
at every height up into the ceiling
(thatched with a brown straw held back by beams
of rough timber knotted with dirty corks)
a forest of hushed, fantastic icons
maintain a watch: violins,
in every complexion a tree could imagine,
of gold, caramel, brown and red,
suspend the cottage, and of all magnitudes
from tenth to full, and violas too,
even a cello in its corner sulk—
and there are the bows to break up the design
like random bar-lines, and a committee
of music-stands by the shy chimney
next to the piano black with humility,
its lid ajar and its keys, from a distance,
a luminous strip of infinity and truth
simmering in the dusky room like heat.
And as the eyes slowly accustom themselves
and the ears tune in to the silence
and to the universe hung behind it
and as the fingers twitch and the tongue
    pauses for breath
and the entering air fetches the elegant resins
and the dizzy fragrance of wood, varnish, glue,
and the senses begin to construct their own instrument

and the room starts to rotate, ever so slowly,
and the eyes accustom themselves
and the man is speaking...

'The universe makes no sense without music.'

He shuffles round the room, but *legato*,
adjusting the tilt of a bow, the bend of a scroll,
he flicks a speck of dust from a fingerboard,
blows at another, flourishes a thumb
to trace the curve of a thick configuration
of figures in the corner by the writing-desk,
jabs his spectacles up off the bridge
of his nose and double-stops at the stove
where a score unfolds
into a music-stand charged with patience,
selects a rich violin, fondly nestles it
into his shoulder and his chin. 'I shall play you
a new Romance by Beethoven, or perhaps
a waltz by Komdy or Lugubrianov—

see if you can tell.'

The line is honey, the intonation—
almost the razor Viotti can wield
or the Concertmaster at the Court Opera—
brushes the room with ribbons of colour
that float to the floorboards, drift to the rafters
and shred the silence into fragments of thought
and shape into questions that can never be answered
but with questions that can never be answered.
His knuckles pulsate and his wrist is swimming

upstream through oil, down through geometry,
upward again. The chamber is turning.
                                        He laughs
up at the imaginary gods, he laughs
and lays down the music.

    Was it a minute, a week, an hour?
A pair of flames in twin candelabra
stands on the piano next to the chimney
and darkness is burning from outside the window
and time has visited
and something has happened
        but everything, nothing is altered.

    He shuffles, a secret smile in his beard,
the eyes are hillocked by the staved old brow
planted with tufts of occasional hair,
the bulbous nose will menace the lip
protruding moist and red and convivial,
the ears are missing, hidden abruptly
by a leathery cap that suddenly gleams
                                on his skull;
and the spectacles glide to the bench
by the rocking-chair
next to a book bent to its aging,
its cover foxed and mottled with stains,
its blocking in ancient gold unreadable
in the dim room's darkening clutter,
in the violin room he is leaving.

III

Let us walk back now,
let us walk back to the city of time,
let us abandon the violin-maker
making his circuits around the cottage
clunking about with rods and buckets
collecting his daily chores.
We turn to regard him for one last moment,
the grasses lift to drown his figure,
he waves as if from another dimension,
a peculiar music is rising around us,
the cottage is sinking back in its valley,
we walk along a peculiar music,
walk back to the city of time.

Turn once again: all is now forest,
the house we visited never existed.
We plunge deep into the murmuring forest:
a sparrow forges a tall parabola,
a beam of daylight showers a clearing,
toadstools burn like huddling reflectors,
tree-trunks sway in their bleakest wisdom,
the wisdom of time, the wisdom of waiting
expecting nothing—a woodlark, a cuckoo,
a caterpillar hangs from a twitching leaf,
the pathway thickens, the clearings darken,
the leaves we are treading obey devoutly,
the forest darkens, we stop.

Somewhere beyond, a railroad glistens,
a mound that runs like an inverse river
from one horizon into another
across a green and yellowing century—
wheatfields, poppyfields, sunflowers sleeping,
the wading farmboys, the colourful women
in billowing skirts and ribbons that flutter
their Maypole colours for locomotives
that drag the city across these pastures,
whistle its warning and dwindle again.
And somewhere beyond, the farmhouses squatting,
their chimneys measuring out the minutes,
their breathing silent and safe.

But we will not push beyond the forest,
the forest contains all we desire,
the city of time with its clocks and archways
can wait, continue, we are alone here:
we are alone with the murmuring forest—
we are complete, time is invisible.

And now a question rises, hovers,
the creatures vanish as if to listen,
the branches pause, the tree-trunks heave
a breath as deep as the endless forest,
the sky is a shimmer of leaves regrouping—
an answer forms. Somewhere beyond,
an ancient artisan stops and chuckles.
You shoulder the fiddle and play.

The Monitor

Matthew Karpin

Matthew Karpin is a Sydney-born writer who remembers the rabbi at school referring, with dismay, to 'the notorious Karpins'. His first novel is In Our Own Day. *His next, to be published by New Endeavour Press, will be a tragicomedy called* The Thesis. *Recent short stories by him can be read in* Imago *and forthcoming issues of* Siglo *magazine. Last year he completed a Varuna fellowship. He is now working, in Armidale, on a novel entitled* The Giants. *'The Monitor' is an extract from a novel also called* The Monitor.

AT SIXTEEN PAST SIX in the morning I woke up, in no sense the right time but since falling ill I'd kept very strange hours, and recalled that the night before Rebecca had walked out on me during an argument, slamming the front door as she left. I lay undisturbed in unchanged sheets until nine o'clock. But right at that hour, on the hour, according to the bedroom digital clock—bearing in mind that I didn't know if it was totally accurate and had in fact known it at times when I hadn't adjusted it for some days to be as much as a minute and many seconds wrong— I heard the front door being unlocked and realised she was coming home at last, that I could relax, have something to eat, someone to change my sheets and turn the lights on and off, as was appropriate given the time of day or night, while I remained in bed.

*

I'd begun a new life as a media monitor two years earlier, a job which enforced a rigid schedule both at work and at home. It meant I had to get up at ten past five in the morning, leaving just enough time to do my two-minute exercises, take my shower where I also shaved, wash my hair every second day, dress in the dark so that I wouldn't

wake Rebecca, put on the clothes for the same reason carefully laid out the night before, the long johns in winter,
underpants, socks and handkerchief, each item beautifully
clean, obtain three tissues from the box in the kitchen to
go with a handkerchief, more of course if I had a cold, hay
fever, or sinus trouble, the correct white shirt which was
one of five that I wore twice before washing, such a system
possible only with the proper use of a deodorant, arranged
in order on the clothes horse so that I couldn't accidentally
wear the same shirt twice in a row before it was due, eat
breakfast while listening to the first radio news in order to
get the jump on the job, that is, mental notes, and leave
the apartment at thirteen past six precisely in case the ele-
vator coming to me on the eighth floor took a full eighteen
seconds to arrive, which could, in effect, throw me out for
the entire day.

Once at the office I recorded my arrival in the atten-
dance book to the minute, even though no one else did. If
need be I'd then also require time to go to the toilet, right
out of the office and down the corridor, because according
to the routine my bowels and bladder might be working,
and there was no alternative. But I had to be straight back
at my post, adjacent to the deck of cassette recorders, when
the buzzer went off at one minute to seven, so that I could
silence it and put down fresh tapes to record the news and
programs from all fifteen radio stations across the board at
seven o'clock.

My schedule consisted entirely of complex programs,
those that would have stumped the other monitors if they
had been required to summarise them and enter them
into the database for our clients. But I'd risen to the

considerable challenge, responsible for monitoring four half-hours of the best and most popular announcer on radio, Peter Riley, a man who spoke quickly and passionately and with such compulsive force that I was in fact addicted to him and would have had to listen to him in my spare time at home if it hadn't been my duty at work.

*

The Monday of the week I fell ill, my monitoring began with a very serious report that I knew would dominate news and talkback shows all day. I typed the first line of the report into the database verbatim: 'The federal government is to review next year's immigration policy as the result of an inquiry which has found that by the end of this decade some of our larger cities may not be able to cope with the current two per cent population growth rate'.

Once the news was over, Peter Riley advanced his program with extraordinary vigour, more than usually upset this morning about the immigration issue.

ANNOUNCER: As you know I've been to the new casino in Melbourne and I'm glad I went. I have to tell you that while I was there the place was thick with Asians and, I might add, none too carefully dressed. Some had slapped on maybe a tee shirt and thongs, a pair of shorts. (*Laughing.*) There is not too much formality among that lot, I can assure you. But they also seemed to have plenty of money, I can assure you of *that*. Where in God's name does all their money come from? It was like a bank, I saw bundles of notes. (*Laughing again*.) The place was literally swarming with these people, that's for sure, and the careful use of soap and brushes would not have gone astray in that crowd. The ones I spoke to I discovered all had names like Hung Yao or Tai Pun, or whatever. There wasn't a single Australian name among them, barely a single white face to be seen. I felt out of place. You would have heard the report in the news just a moment ago that immigration numbers in Sydney are now seriously out of control. In light of this, I think it is appropriate to ask the federal immigration minister what *are* the government's policies, what is going to be done about overcrowding? And what do you, the ordinary listener out there, think about all of this? Give us a call.

I began monitoring the second half-hour of Peter Riley's program in which he spoke to callers.

FEMALE TALKBACK CALLER: I'd like to comment on Asian immigration in this country. I really think that for far too long ordinary people have been silent about what's happening. I don't believe that the government has any right to inflict all of these free-loaders from other countries onto our community. This used to be a very quiet, happy and peaceful place to live and work. I remember things as they were when I was a child, and now look at the place. Wherever you go there's an Asian fellow or a dark fellow.

ANNOUNCER: Now come on, give them a fair go. Let's not tar all these people with the same brush, we're not into that business yet, I hope. Some Asians have come into our community quite legitimately, some even came here many generations ago and have produced a great deal of wealth for the community.

FEMALE TALKBACK CALLER: But we're talking at cross purposes! I am just talking about the Asians, the Indians, the Negroes, whoever, who come here from their second and third rate countries, apparently with our government's blessing. When they get here, they bludge off our social security. They don't get a job, they don't even try. They never intended to. They came here in the first place to take advantage of our country's wealth. It's a disgrace.

ANNOUNCER: Well, yes, *those* people, and as we all know there are some, undoubtedly in fact there are many, whether or not we are prepared to admit it, and in many cases political correctness constrains *others* from speaking out against this sort of thing, but I hope will never prevent me, those people should never have been allowed into the country in the first place.

MALE TALKBACK CALLER: Last weekend my son, fourteen years old, a very respectable boy who would never harm anyone, was attacked by a gang of these yellow hooligans on the train. (*Starting to cry.*)

ANNOUNCER: The poor man.

MALE TALKBACK CALLER: He struggled home afterwards, all on his own, but he was badly beaten up by these yellow bastards, and given a broken arm. They don't even belong in this country, so what are they doing here? They don't share our beliefs. I just think it's terrible. We've let criminal elements into our society which endanger our own children. An absolute disgrace! I think a lot of their money comes from organised crime. We've all heard of the Chinese mafia, and now we've let it into our country.

ANNOUNCER: The poor man. You're absolutely right of course, it is a disgrace. Australia was a civilised country where we had achieved some great things since our arrival just over two hundred years ago. But now we have enough problems of our own without actually importing crime. You are quite right. Just stay on the line for a moment, would you, you unfortunate man, because we might get some further details from you. I'd like to do something to help you out.

*

Now as I lay ill in bed, the immigration debate of three days earlier had faded from my memory—but I was about to discover just how close to home it had in fact come. Although Rebecca had returned at last, strangely even several minutes after she opened the front door she hadn't actually come into the bedroom to see me. From the next room I heard the muffled sound of banging and dragging, things falling over, and unbelievably for a moment it seemed I heard another, foreign voice, which I thought I knew. The strange noises became a matter of considerable concern, but just before I was going to simply get up to have a look, the bedroom door opened sharply and who should march in but Than, a Vietnamese friend of Rebecca's I had met once before.

'You don't get up,' he said looking over me, '*so* sick,' and I noted the tone of sarcasm.

'What the hell are you doing here?' I asked. 'Where the hell is Rebecca?'

'I'm out here, Michael,' her voice called out, 'packing up some of my stuff.'

I exclaimed in a way that, when I now think about it, must have only added to Than's triumph, who began to round on me in a language that in all truth was barely comprehensible, some absurd combination of his language and mine, how, 'You bastard, you think you very good, Mr Monitor, your *English language*. Well, your wife leave you and come to me now, the Asian wog, but still much better than you. I am not always sick, I am not—' the word he meant was 'obsessive'—'I make things happen even in this country. We have children, a life, and I get some real money.'

I called out to Rebecca, demanding that she come into the bedroom to translate the gibberish, which she finally did, reluctantly, to tell me, 'What he's saying is true, Michael, more or less. You and I have really run our course together. I can't live with you any more, I'm going to live with Than. That's why I've been moving out the things that belong to me,' and then she walked out of the room again.

But even after she left Than remained standing over me, saying, 'Little white Australian bastard! You so good, yes, well you not good enough for Rebecca, she come to me now, she come to *gook*!' and would have continued for many more minutes in exactly this way, I am sure, throwing his arms about and abusing me while standing right there next to my own bed as I lay speechless, except that Rebecca returned to the bedroom and pulled him away, closing the door behind him. I lay frozen in bed and devastated, listening to more boxes being packed, the removal continuing in the living room as Than evidently helped her pack her belongings and, for all I knew, many of *my* belongings, so that she could get away from me and go and live with him, just like that. When finally they had both left at last, one hour and twenty-seven minutes after they first arrived, I dragged myself out of bed into the next room to see what had happened and discovered that most of the books were gone, as were the television, the stereo and the couch, and when I looked in the kitchen I saw that every last pot and pan had been removed. And I realised that it was true what they all say, the bloody Asians are getting into our country, literally into our houses, and robbing us blind while our backs are turned.

With that realisation I went straight back to bed in a state of outrage instead of the despair I should and would otherwise have felt in more normal circumstances, if I had not just been robbed *blind*. For several unrecorded hours and minutes I tried to concentrate on this thought while I suffered increasing nausea, reminding myself that an Asian person had robbed me blind while I lay sick in bed, as they were in fact continually robbing this country, as growing numbers of people were experiencing, but soon I couldn't forget the other thing that had happened, that after five long years Rebecca had walked out on me.

It was fourteen to ten according to the digital clock when the second realisation first struck home, conveying with it also the idea that everything was pointless, the time itself that was ticking away, never to be recalled, so point-less that it marked nothing but itself. It was thirteen to ten and impossible to deal with this. Coping with the millions of minutes left would be beyond me because I'd have to do it on my own, I would never be able even to go back to work in this state, and with Rebecca gone I would be noth-ing but a wreck. I already was a wreck. Not knowing what to do, I turned over and over in bed. Twelve to ten. I couldn't go on for the rest of my life simply counting the minutes, never sleeping or eating, and just watching time go by. I couldn't even bear to do that until I was well enough to go back to work, which on my best estimates would amount to another 4395 minutes. It was eleven to ten. What could I do?

But then, in my despair, I scanned the bedroom and in the corner of my eye caught sight of a very unremarkable object, my bedroom radio. It occurred to me that, although I could not be at work to monitor the media, I could after all do the same thing at home, if I chose. I had my radio for comfort and companionship and I could listen to the middle of Simon Ancek's show. Ten to ten.

ANNOUNCER: If you've only just joined the show, we're talking about a very unpleasant issue today. The sub-ject is domestic violence, and what causes it. The simple explanation, of course, is neanderthal husbands and their whingeing wives. And if you're particularly unlucky, a handful of brats.

FEMALE TALKBACK CALLER: Simon, I wanted to talk about domestic violence with you. My story is a little tragic. I only hope I don't start crying.

ANNOUNCER: My God, you're not the only one. Don't start crying, dear.

FEMALE TALKBACK CALLER: Well, I'll try not to. About eight-and-a-half years ago my daughter married a man against the advice of my husband and myself. I don't know why she did it or what attracted her to him in the first place. She was a small thing, and very delicate. He was a very big and heavyset man, foreign, twice my daughter's weight. He used to get angry for no apparent reason, and at the time we thought maybe because he didn't speak very good English he needed to vent his frustration. But he'd get violent and take it out on her. He often used foul language and lost his temper in front of us. But four years ago today he shot my daughter dead and then shot himself. We never even had a chance to say goodbye to our beautiful daughter.

ANNOUNCER: That *is* a tragic story, and we can only hope that if anyone out there from the federal government is listening they'll pay attention. This story is a direct consequence of all the ridiculous immigration policies that have been foisted on this country.

Now, let's take another call.

FEMALE TALKBACK CALLER: I know it sounds hard, but I actually don't have any sympathy for your last caller or her daughter who was killed. I really think most people bring their own misfortune on themselves. If she was married to a violent man, why didn't she leave him? Why did she marry him in the first place? You have to ask these questions.

MALE TALKBACK CALLER: I'm actually a counsellor and I see battered women every day. I actually find it hard to face the new day, knowing all the crises I am going to be confronted with when I get into the office in the morning.

ANNOUNCER: What kind of men commit the terrible acts that we've just heard our caller describe?

MALE TALKBACK CALLER: All sorts of men really. It always amazes me how on the one hand you can have a man who's a really good mate in the pub, where everyone likes him. He really has no apparent problems with friendship in that context. But when he gets home, drunk, his behaviour can change completely and he beats up his wife, or he sexually abuses his own daughter. It's just horrifying.

ANNOUNCER: Yes, but do you find it's men with some real problem of their own who are more often offenders? For some reason they are unable or unwilling to cope?

MALE TALKBACK CALLER: These men look and act normal most of the time.

ANNOUNCER: But is there a sign a woman could use, a sign of incompatibility perhaps, that could warn her about a particular man she was becoming involved with?

MALE TALKBACK CALLER: That can be the case, yes, often, if there is a big social, economic or cultural gulf between the partners when they get together, that in itself can definitely lead to problems.

ANNOUNCER: So, if one partner is, for example, Aboriginal or Asian, and the other is an average white person, that could in itself be asking for trouble?

MALE TALKBACK CALLER: Well, Simon, that can definitely be the basis for much heartache.

ANNOUNCER: It's really only common sense, isn't it?

I was affected by everything being discussed and realised that Rebecca was in more trouble than she was yet aware. Her friend Than was obviously the violent type. I'd felt very threatened when he stood over me as I lay in bed, and she may have gone with him today but sooner or later she would be back. However, it was no longer enough for me alone to know this, I wanted to share my story, and so, deciding at last to be brave and telephone Simon Ancek myself, I staggered out to the living room and brought the telephone into the bedroom. I rang the six-digit number and was put on hold. I waited twenty minutes and eighteen seconds, sweating it out, when without warning Simon Ancek's voice broke through, talking directly to me.

ANNOUNCER: Michael, hello.

MICHAEL MACKENZIE: Hello Simon. Simon, I wanted to talk about my own personal situation, if that's allright. I was in a happy marriage for many years. Things were going along very smoothly and I couldn't have asked for more. But suddenly—as a matter of fact just earlier today—she left me. She moved out with another person. And she really hit me while I was down. You see, I'm also not at all well. I've been sick now for four days. But the real problem is, she's moved out with this Asian man she's been seeing behind my back.

ANNOUNCER: Well, we are talking about domestic violence today, you moron.

MICHAEL MACKENZIE: Yes, I know, but it could lead to that. You see, the person she's seeing is Asian. He can barely even speak English. She once had him over for dinner and it was impossible to have a conversation. He couldn't speak a word of English. So we just sat there.

ANNOUNCER: Look, Michael, I'm going to cut you off. We can do without your racist comments on this program, thank you. You really *are* a pathetic excuse for a man, aren't you? Why are you wasting my air time? What does it say, to you, that she chose to leave you for him? Have you asked yourself that question? You're an idiot I'm afraid, a fool…

And he hung up on me, leaving me there, sick in bed with the telephone still in my hand, worse than ever. I hadn't even thought of his interpretation, that it said nothing for me that my wife had left me for an Asian. As it turned out, I wasn't one of the good people regularly praised by radio broadcasters, the battlers and those who had to try hard, those who never really make up any ground in their lives and always have to work extremely hard for what they *do* get. I was instead another one of the idiots always ridiculed over the air, those with the wrong opinions about everything, who don't understand the real ways of the world, and have everything too easily or nothing at all—while at the same time deserving nothing.

I lay back in bed while Simon Ancek's voice continued, hungry, derided and in despair, not knowing how I could go on.

Dozing off, I woke up again from a feverish sleep to realise that I'd left the radio on and Simon Ancek's show was now over while Peter Riley's was just beginning. Perhaps Peter Riley would be able to help me where Simon Ancek was unable. I dialled the number for the program and this time I was put on hold for one hour and twenty-five minutes before the announcer spoke to me.

ANNOUNCER: Michael, hello, hello Michael?

MICHAEL MACKENZIE: Hello Peter. There's something I wanted to share with you and your listeners. But it's not very good news really. For the last four days I've been in a terrible slump. I've been depressed and so ill, I haven't even been able to go to work. You see my wife left me today and she really hit me while I was down. (*Starting to cry.*) I haven't been able to cope, I don't know what to do.

ANNOUNCER: Oh you poor man. You're obviously a battler, aren't you? I guess you don't earn very much and normally you can be relied on to work very hard, can't you?

MICHAEL MACKENZIE: I always get up at ten past five to go to work. I never get enough sleep.

ANNOUNCER: Dear oh dear. Well, look, I really only have a single piece of advice for you and for any other person out there also in your situation. It might sound like easy advice but in reality it's very difficult to follow, and it's this. Although life may be extremely hard from time to time, perhaps even all the time if you're really hard up—and I know many of my listeners are—you just have to struggle on. No matter how hard it may get, work is the most ennobling thing I know of. You just have to redouble your efforts in the face of all the adversity. When hardship affects you, lose yourself in your job, whatever it may be, whether it's as an important executive somewhere in a top company, or as the secretary or cleaner for the same organisation. It's simply what you've got to do. It's the *only* thing you really have to do.

I got off the telephone after he finished and for a moment fell back into bed. His advice was right of course, and just what I needed to hear.

*

When my alarm sounded at ten past five in the morning I didn't waste a second but got straight out of bed, even though I felt ill in my stomach. I was determined to return completely to routine, more strictly than ever before, and if any extraneous thoughts intruded, push myself harder to ignore them. Work was ennobling, the only thing I knew that was. By ten past six, just as the second hand came up to the top of my watch, I was ready as scheduled, and stepped out of the apartment. On the bus, it was important to remain calm when the driver delivered me to my stop eight minutes and twenty-five seconds late. I sprinted from there to the office, making up two minutes and ten seconds, so that I walked to my desk puffing.

Thirty minutes after my arrival I found I was running only eight seconds off schedule, in spite of the intrusion of thoughts of Rebecca, but there was no time even to think of that or I would lose any advantage I'd gained. At one point I began to think I can't possibly go on, my wife has left me, I have hardly any furniture left, everything is as good as lost, but I heard the voice of Peter Riley, 'You have to struggle on, no matter how hard it may get', and I realised that that attitude is what makes our country work, as it does in all the other countries in the civilised world, and if not for losing yourself in work, in the grind, being addicted to the schedule, we would all just give up and not bother, it wouldn't be possible to have created our culture, our sort of people, our race. It was what, after all, I had seen my own parents do, and it was the only reason I had advanced even as far as I had, but as soon as I fell off track and forgot my schedule, I would be in trouble again.

As I typed as fast as I could, keeping up with and out-doing all the other monitors, I had good reason to believe that the experiences of the past week, so calamitous at the time and ending with my two defining telephone calls to the radio announcers themselves, had actually been of great benefit because, the day continuing, minute by minute, I found myself for the first time ever adhering exactly to my schedule. But then, three hours and sixteen minutes into the day's work, having just checked my watch, it suddenly, incongruously, began to seem as though I had been picked up by a huge wave that was drawing closer and closer to the shore, only to drag me back out, after dumping me, into the ocean of work.

Glossary

Bar Mitzvah (Hebrew)—a rite of passage which bestows manhood on a thirteen-year-old boy; he then becomes responsible for his religious deeds

blintz (Yiddish)—a pancake, usually filled with cream cheese and raisins

broygis (Yiddish)—angry, upset, sullen

Chanukah (Hebrew)—a Jewish festival occurring in December, which celebrates the victory of a Jewish army against the Greeks in 522 BC. Also known as the Festival of Lights.

echt (German)—the genuine article, the real McCoy

gefilte fish (German)—fish balls, chopped or ground and mixed with eggs, salt, onions and pepper. Tradition Friday night fare, served at the Sabbath dinner

hora   (Hebrew)—a traditional Jewish folk-dance

Kaddish (Hebrew)—a memorial prayer for the dead

kashrut (Hebrew)—refers to the correct preparation of food and slaughter of animals in accordance with traditional Jewish law. Better known as 'keeping *kosher*'.

kibbutz (Yiddish)—a cooperative agricultural community in Israel. Many today have an industrial or hospitality component

klops (Yiddish)—meatloaf

latkes (Yiddish)—potato pancakes, traditional Central European Jewish food

lokshen (Yiddish)—noodles

mammaloshen (Yiddish)—literally, mother language or mother tongue. Refers to Yiddish itself

meshugenah (Yiddish)—crazy; a person who is *meshugah* (crazy)

minyan (Hebrew)—minimum number (ten) of males required for religious service to be conducted. No congregational prayers or rites can begin until there is a *minyan*.

mitzvah-tensl (Yiddish)—a wedding dance, traditionally performed by the bride and groom

naches (Yiddish)—pride, special joy, particularly from the achievements of a child

nu (Russian/Yiddish)—literally, 'well', 'well now'. One of the most frequently used words in Yiddish. A remarkably versatile word, it can be used as an interjection, interrogation or expletive

Rosh Hashonah (Hebrew)—Jewish New Year

Shabbat (Hebrew)—the Sabbath

Shabbes (Yiddish)—the Sabbath

shalom (Hebrew)—a traditional Jewish greeting or salutation. Literally means peace

shiva (Hebrew)—period of mourning. To 'sit *shiva*' means to sit in mourning for seven days after the death of a loved one

shleper (Yiddish)—one who has to carry or drag something (usually a heavy object)

Shoah (Hebrew)—the Hebrew term for the Holocaust

shpilkes (Yiddish)—anxiety; to be on edge, on tenterhooks

shtetl (Yiddish)—a Jewish village in pre-war Poland/ Ukraine

shul (Yiddish)—synagogue or house of prayer

tuches (Yiddish)—backside; as in famous expression: 'kiss my *tuches*'

Yeshiva (Hebrew)—refers to either or both the following: a house of religious study; a rabbinical training school

Yom Kippur (Hebrew)—Holiest day in the Jewish year. The day of Atonement during which Jews are required to fast. Occurs ten days after New Year

WIZO—acronym for Women's International Zionist Organisation. Raises money for Israel and for charity

Acknowledgments

Part of 'Only Connect' by Andrea Goldsmth first appeared as 'Talmudic Excursions' in *Westerly*, December 1996; Ramona Koval's piece, 'Samovar', is an extract from her novel, *Samovar*, published by Minerva, 1996; 'But is he Jewish?' by Elisabeth Wynhausen is an extract taken from her novel, *Manly Girls*, published by Penguin, 1989; Arnold Zable's piece 'You Cannot Imagine' is an extract from his book, *Jewels and Ashes*, published by Scribe, 1991; 'Things Could be Worse' by Lily Brett is a short story from her anthology, *Things Could Be Worse*, published by Meanjin/Melbourne University Press, 1990; Bernard Cohen's piece 'Breitbart, the Strongest Jew' first appeared in *Westerly*, December 1996; 'Hopscotch' by Brian Castro first appeared in the anthology, *A Sporting Declaration*, edited by Manfred Jurgensen, published by Phoenix, 1996; Ron Elisha's piece 'Paris' is an extract from an unpublished novel, *Paris*; permission to reproduce 'The Wailing Wall' and 'Hot Date' by Dorothy Porter from Hyland House; permission to reproduce the extract from *The Fiftieth Gate* (1997) by Mark Baker from HarperCollins Publisher; permission to reproduce 'Hansel and Gretel', 'On the Way to the Operating Theatre' and 'After the Operation' by Doris Brett from Hale & Iremonger.